BROKEN PIECES TO MASTER PIECES
BECOMING MORE THROUGH BROKENNESS

Dr. Jeffery A. Williams

Broken Pieces to Master Pieces
by Dr. Jeffery A. Williams
Copyright © 2024 Dr. Jeffery A. Williams

All rights reserved. This book is protected under the copyright laws of the United States of America. This book may not be copied or reprinted for commercial gain or profit.

Unless otherwise identified, Scripture quotations are taken from THE AMPLIFIED BIBLE © 2015 by The Lockman Foundation, La Habra, CA 90631. All rights reserved.

Scripture quotations marked KJV are taken from the KING JAMES VERSION and rest in the public domain.

Scripture quotations marked CJB are taken from the COMPLETE JEWISH BIBLE. Copyright © 1998 by David H. Stern. All rights reserved.

Scripture quotations marked NIV are taken from THE HOLY BIBLE, NEW INTERNATIONAL VERSION®, NIV® Copyright © 1973, 1978, 1984, 2011 by Biblica, Inc.® Used by permission. All rights reserved worldwide.

ISBN 978-1-63360-283-0

For Worldwide Distribution
Printed in the USA

Urban Press
P.O. Box 8881
Pittsburgh, PA 15221-0881
412.646.2780

Dedication

In honor of my father, Alfonso Williams Jr., a selfless family man whose unwavering faith and fidelity to my mother, Lillie Williams, defined their 67-year marriage. As an entrepreneur , musician, and athlete, he exemplified what it means to be a loving husband and devoted father to four children, as well as a proud grandfather to three grandchildren. He truly embodied the measure of a man.

December 24, 1936 - July 20, 2023

"Now the man Moses was very meek (gentle, kind, and humble) or above all the men on the face of the earth" (Numbers 12:3).

"His master said to him, 'Well done, you upright (honorable, admirable) and faithful servant!'" (Matthew 25:21).

Contents

Preface	ix
Introduction	xi

Chapter 1:
The Ways of God — 1

Chapter 2
What's Got You? — 6

Chapter 3
What Are You After? — 12

Chapter 4
A Different View of Holiness — 16

Chapter 5
Caution – Contains Broken Pieces — 19

Chapter 6
Nothing Broken, Nothing Missing — 23

Chapter 7
The Cost of Blessing — 28

Chapter 8
The Necessity of Obedience for Blessing — 31

Chapter 9
**The Garden of Gethsemane –
The Place of Breaking** — 36

Chapter 10
The Intimate Encounter in the Garden — 40

Chapter 11
The Best Part Is on the Inside You — 44

Chapter 12
Because Broken Is Better — 48

Chapter 13
One Look Can Change Your Life — 52

Chapter 14
Imitate to Replicate — 55

Chapter 15
Look Up If You Want Heaven to Come Down — 58

Chapter 16
Closer To Home — 62

Chapter 17
**Heavenly Perspective and
Fragments of Grace** — 66

Chapter 18 **Distribution of Brokenness and Embracing Inadequacy**	69
Chapter 19 **I Want To See Jesus**	73
Chapter 20 **I Saw It In My Own Life**	77
Chapter 21 **Are We There Yet?**	80
Chapter 22 **Signs of True Brokenness**	84
Chapter 23 **What Brokenness is Not**	87
Chapter 24 **Broken People**	91
Chapter 25 **He Only Uses Broken People**	95
Chapter 26 **Jesus Blessed What He Broke And Gave Only What Was Broken**	101
Chapter 27 **A Broken Revelation**	106
Chapter 28 **School's in Session – Six Takeaways on Embracing Brokenness**	109
Chapter 29 **Ten Insights to Embracing Wholeness**	113
Chapter 30 **The Journey from Brokenness to Purposeful Transformation**	117
Chapter 31 **There's A Master Piece In There**	121

"My [only] sacrifice [acceptable] to God is a broken spirit; a broken and contrite heart [broken with sorrow for sin, thoroughly penitent], such, O God, You will not despise" – Psalm 51:17

The apostles [who had been sent out on a mission] gathered together with Jesus and told Him everything that they had done and taught. He said to them, "Come away by yourselves to a secluded place and rest a little while"—for there were many [people who were continually] coming and going, and they could not even find time to eat. And they went away by themselves in the boat to a secluded place. Many [people] saw them leaving, and recognized them and ran there together on foot from all the [surrounding] cities, and got there ahead of them. When Jesus went ashore, He saw a large crowd [waiting], and He was moved with compassion for them because they were like sheep without a shepherd [lacking guidance]; and He began to teach them many things. When the day was nearly gone, His disciples came to Him and said, "This is an isolated place, and it is already late; send the crowds away so that they may go into the surrounding countryside and villages and buy themselves something to eat."

But He replied, "You give them something to eat!" And they asked Him, "Shall we go and buy 200 denarii worth of bread and give it to them to eat?" He said to them, "How many loaves do you have? Go look!" And when they found out, they said, "Five [loaves], and two fish." Then Jesus commanded them all to sit down by groups on the green grass. They sat down in groups of hundreds and of fifties [so that the crowd resembled an orderly arrangement of colorful garden plots]. Taking the five loaves and two fish, He looked up to heaven and said a blessing [of praise and thanksgiving to the Father]. Then He broke the loaves and [repeatedly] gave them to the disciples to set before the people; and He divided up the two fish among them all. They all ate and were satisfied. And the disciples picked up twelve full baskets of the broken pieces [of the loaves], and of the fish. Those who ate the loaves were five thousand men [not counting the women and children].
– Mark 6:30-44

Preface

I embarked on the journey of writing this book with one purpose in mind: to offer guidance to others navigating life's trials, showing them that in the face of adversity, we can emerge stronger and are capable of achieving more by learning to tap into a miraculous power that manifests in our darkest moments. The genesis of this book can be traced back fifteen years ago when I delivered a sermon titled "Broken Pieces," laying the foundation for what you're about to read.

It was a profound revelation that sustained me through an excruciating period when it felt like everything I held dear was either broken or on the brink of shattering. This message, coupled with transformative insights gleaned from my previous book, *Knowing Your WHY: Key to Unlocking Your Full Potential,* which I self-published in 2015, played a pivotal role in revitalizing my spirit.

I found myself grappling with severe clinical depression amidst the dissolution of an 18-year marriage, the sudden loss of my youngest sister, Linelle, the tragic passing of a passionate young ministry associate, and the weight of substantial financial debt. As the Apostle Paul said, "and the concern of all the churches" (2 Corinthians 11:28), was added to my pressures. All this happened while pursuing my doctor of ministry degree (in the thesis writing phase) and shepherding one of the fastest-growing churches in southern New England. Yet, quitting was never an option. With two pre-teen daughters depending on me for strength, security, and guidance, finding a way through was my top priority.

Another motivation for writing this book stemmed from my quest for significance and meaning, particularly as I entered the "second half" of my life. Wrestling with whether I had maximized the opportunities afforded me, I found solace in exploring profound truths from the story of Jesus miraculously feeding over 5,000 people with just five barley loaves and two fish—broken pieces.

I pondered, *Could the Lord do something similar with the fragments of my own life? Would He multiply the time I have left on this earth to fulfill His assigned purpose? What was the significance of Jesus blessing the broken bread, breaking it further, and multiplying its power to nourish those who remained to hear His message? If something is broken, how can it bring healing and wholeness to others? Most importantly, how could this ancient story speak to my brokenness?*

This book offers insights, spiritual guidance, and meaningful answers to life's pressing questions. Drawing from personal experience and deep reflections on timeless truths, it illuminates a path toward healing, purpose, and a deeper connection with the God of the Bible as you walk through your own trials and challenges

    Bishop Jeffery A. Williams
    Providence, Rhode Island
    October 2024

Introduction

The term "brokenness" evokes many emotions like pain, loss, disappointment—all familiar to human experience. While not a comfortable topic, brokenness touches every life at some point. However, I want to clarify that this work isn't a glorification of the trials believers like you face, whether they emanate from human or demonic sources. Nor is it a call to embrace difficulties to offer excellent service to God. Instead, it explores the pivotal role of brokenness in allowing God to work through us more effectively. We discover that we can achieve extraordinary things by diminishing ourselves, as illustrated in the gospel of Mark, chapter 6.

At first glance, the story in Mark 6 may appear to focus solely on Jesus miraculously feeding thousands with only a few loaves and fish. Yet upon closer examination, it reveals numerous personal insights and applications beyond the surface narrative. Similarly, multiplication at the hands of Jesus is also seen during a wedding He attended in Cana of Galilee. At this wedding, Jesus' mother approached Him to solve a problem: the wine was all gone! During this celebratory time, Jesus turned water into the finest wine possible.

Though this writing focuses on bread and fish, we would be short-sighted to believe that the revelatory truth contained in both stories was limited to a benign magic trick to avoid embarrassment for those who hosted the nuptials. Instead, we have a precious opportunity and duty to ask the Holy Spirit for insight to properly apply the truths that lie just below the obvious. *Broken Pieces* is my attempt to uncover some of the deeper truths of the story and how they relate to our lives, revealing how brokenness is the starting point for wholeness.

The application of this event isn't confined to miracles of bread and fish, the basics of human existence. Rather, it speaks to the very essence of our faith journey. We're given a sacred opportunity to seek insights beyond the surface, guided by the Holy Spirit. *Broken Pieces* delves into these deeper truths and their relevance for our lives, urging us to engage with Scripture in a way that will not just inform but also transform. As we embark on this journey, let's not settle for surface-level interpretations of familiar biblical stories. Instead, let's embrace the call to go deeper and seek divine revelation and practical application.

Broken Pieces is a shining pillar, illuminating the path toward a richer understanding of God's workings through our brokenness. At the end of each chapter, you will find a series of "Reflection Questions," designed to help you consider the truths within the chapter and gain more understanding of your faith journey and the role brokenness plays in your life. Here's a sample as we close this introduction:

Reflection Question

What does personal "brokenness" mean to you?

You may want to journal your thoughts as you meditate on that question. Or you may wish to go through *Broken Pieces* with others, and this question can serve to guide your discussions. However you utilize them, I pray you won't skip over them so you can get to the next chapter and finish the book. God has something to say to you through this presentation, and I want you to maximize its impact. You will never be the same once you understand how God will use your broken pieces to create master pieces that will sustain you and nourish others.

And now, let's get started with our study and understanding of the how *Broken Pieces* are the keys to your development in the Lord, His means to create His Master Pieces of which you are one.

Chapter 1

The Ways of God

The prophet Isaiah wrote, "His (God's) ways are not our ways" (Isaiah 55:8). How and why God does what He does is often not how we would approach the same matter. The comforting reality is that the All-Knowing God has a great plan (in both scope and quality) for your life. And our present problems haven't surprised God or upset His plan for your life. The truth is that before we were formed in our mother's womb, He knew us (see Jeremiah 1:5; Psalm 139:13). He works all things out according to the counsel of His will (see Ephesians 1:11). The Apostle states in his letter to the Church in Rome, "all things work together for the good of those who love God" (Romans 8:28a).

In other words, before the beginning, before you found yourself in your current predicament(s), your Creator, the God of the heavens had a complete plan for your life which took into careful consideration all the hills, valleys, and turns that would be part of our journey. This thought is best seen in the work of Christ. The Bible tells us that before the foundation of the world was established, the Lamb of God (Jesus Christ) was slain (see Revelation 13:8). His life blood was already shed for our eternal redemption. Amazing.

That tells us that before we were aware of our need to be saved, the Father had already arranged for us to be saved. Before we needed healing, Christ Jesus took the death blows that would eventually bring our complete deliverance. So, your broken life is not a new or insurmountable problem for God. It's something He knew would be part of your life. He didn't cause it. He didn't arrange for it to happen, but He did make provision to mold your wholeness out of the brokenness. However, know with absolute certainty that tragedies, sicknesses, diseases, and the like are never the work of God. How could they be when it was through Christ that we are delivered and healed of these maladies?

It would be inconsistent, not to mention masochistic, for God to put diseases on us, when He clearly stated that Jesus came to make whole all those who come to Him:

> And He went throughout all Galilee, teaching in their synagogues and preaching the good news (gospel) of the kingdom, and healing every kind of disease and every kind of sickness among the people [demonstrating and revealing that He was indeed the promised Messiah] (Matthew 4:23).

In the text found in Mark 6, after blessing the bread, Jesus actually broke it into small pieces. A loaf of bread can be a work of art when it comes out of the oven. However, once it's sliced and broken into pieces, the beauty is lost—although it may have a delicious taste. Jesus changed the look of the bread by breaking it into smaller, bite-size pieces. One can still recognize it as bread, but it is no longer a loaf—instead it's fragments and pieces.

As I will explain later, to an extent, the breaking was necessary to release the full potential trapped within the bread. Although the broken bread is no longer whole, it has the potential now to serve the needs of many people. God will take our lives if we give them to him, and he will break them open and expose the full greatness that has been contained within. This breaking is not done through sickness or tragedy, as some believe, but through a revelation of Himself, His holiness, His goodness. The Apostle Paul wrote,

> Or do you have no regard for the wealth of His kindness and tolerance and patience [in withholding His wrath]? Are you [actually] unaware or ignorant [of the fact] that God's kindness leads you to repentance [that is, to change your inner self, your old way of thinking—seek His purpose for your life]? (Romans 2:4).

Why did He break the bread and not the fish? My thought is simply this. The bread, unlike the fish, was the creation of man. Anything with the unauthorized fingerprints of humanity must be broken, reset if you will. As we will discuss in subsequent chapters, our lives, just like the bread, must be voluntarily entrusted and placed into the hands of Jesus, just as we are—with all the issues, sins, fears, failures, and insecurities. We must allow Him to break us.

The breaking I am describing isn't the breaking that occurs because of our sinful acts and behaviors. Although we can be broken due to our sinful behavior and the evil deeds of others, I'm referring specifically to the dismantling of our own will and way, yielding our lives to the One who died for us as our substitute. Friend, it's in the yielding of our lives that is described in the Scripture, "Then Jesus told his disciples, 'If anyone would come after me, let him deny himself and take up his cross and follow me'" (Matthew 16:24). This is the essence of being a "true Christian."

As you read the Scriptures closely, you will find that Jesus did not refer to those who believed in Him as Christians; instead, they were invited to follow Him, which made them followers. In most churches, at least in North America, we find individuals who believe in the Christian way or ascribe to a Judeo-Christian philosophy. Most have not forsaken their life to follow where Jesus leads. In plain speech, failure to give your life into the Master's hands makes you a peddler of Christian ideals, not a follower of Christ.

The breaking process is the process of transformation and surrender. It is a process that must be voluntarily submitted to, with no promise of ease. It's the moment your will intersects His will, and you give up your will for His will. It is precisely this breaking process that is the precursor and means to continue following Jesus.

Reflection Questions

How do you reconcile the concept of God's sovereignty with the challenges and brokenness you face in life? In other words, if God is all powerful and "in control," what is His role in the trials you face?

Reflect on a time when you felt broken or crushed. How did that experience shape your understanding of God's plan and purpose for your life?

How can you surrender your will and allow God to break and transform you for
His purposes?

Chapter 2

Does It Have You, or Do You Have It?

The parable of the rich young ruler offers profound insights into the human condition and the nature of true discipleship. This young man, as described by Jesus Himself, possessed abundant wealth and was held in high regard by Jesus. Approaching Jesus with earnest questions, he appeared eager to embrace God's ways. Furthermore, he led a morally upright life, diligently adhering to the commandments. Despite these commendable qualities, Jesus identified a critical deficiency: the young man's reluctance to relinquish the worldly possessions that held sway over his heart.

It's crucial to recognize here that Jesus wasn't advocating for universal destitution among His followers. Instead, He pinpointed the young ruler's particular struggle—his attachment to material wealth at the expense of wholehearted devotion to God. The problem was that his riches possessed him, exerting control over his decisions and priorities. When faced with the choice between retaining his earthly treasures and embracing the call to follow Jesus, the young man's allegiance to his possessions eclipsed his commitment to the Son of God, leading him to walk away sorrowfully.

This narrative is a poignant reminder of the inherent tension between our earthly attachments and spiritual aspirations. Like the rich, young ruler, many of us grapple with competing allegiances—wealth, possessions, relationships, or personal ambitions—that vie for prominence in our lives. While these pursuits may not necessarily be sinful, their undue prominence in our hearts can hinder our ability to pursue Christ wholeheartedly. Often, as I have found, when Jesus asks us to give up something, it's because there is something far more valuable that will take its place; *brokenness is the starting point.*

A Tale of Possessions and Responses

At first glance, the stories of the five loaves and two fish and the encounter with the rich young ruler in the Bible might appear unrelated. Yet, upon closer examination, their themes reveal interesting and relevant parallels regarding possessions and responses to Jesus.

In the account of the rich young ruler, we see a man of wealth who approached Jesus seeking eternal life. However, when Jesus instructed him to sell his possessions and give to the poor, the young man's attachment to his wealth outweighed his desire and ability to follow Jesus. His possessions held him back from embracing the call to discipleship, and he departed sorrowful, unable to relinquish what he held dear.

On the other hand, in the story of the five loaves and two fish, we witness a different response to Jesus' call. When faced with feeding a multitude, the disciples initially only saw scarcity—a few loaves and fish amidst a crowd of thousands. Yet, when Jesus asked them to give what they had, they responded in faith, offering their meager provisions. Despite their doubts and reservations, they surrendered their possessions to Jesus.

In both instances, possessions were involved—the rich young ruler held tightly to his wealth, while the disciples offered up their limited provisions. However, the responses to Jesus' call differed greatly, leading to contrasting outcomes. The rich young ruler's attachment to his possessions hindered his ability to follow Jesus wholeheartedly, while the disciples' willingness to give what little they had opened the door to a miraculous multiplication and abundance.

These stories serve as poignant reminders of the significance of our responses to Jesus' invitations in our lives. Do we cling tightly to our possessions, allowing them to dictate our priorities and hinder our relationship with Him? Or do we trust in His provision, even when faced with scarcity, and offer up what we have in faith, knowing that He can multiply it beyond measure? Our choice echoes through eternity, shaping the trajectory of our spiritual journey and our capacity to experience the fullness of life in Christ.

The journey of discipleship demands a radical reordering of priorities—a willingness to relinquish anything threatening to eclipse our devotion to Christ. Brokenness is often a step in the reordering process. Such voluntary surrender constitutes an essential aspect of the spiritual journey as we learn to identify and release the idols that vie for our affection. In the process of yielding to God's lordship, we discover the liberating truth that nothing in this world can compare to the surpassing worth of knowing Christ and experiencing His transformative power in our lives.

In the broader context of Christian discipleship, the call to surrender extends beyond material possessions to encompass every area of our lives. Our ambitions, desires, fears, and insecurities must all be submitted to the refining work of God's Spirit, who reshapes us into vessels fit for His purposes. Although challenging, this process of voluntary breaking paves the way for the outpouring of God's glory through our brokenness, bringing healing and restoration first to us and then through us to a broken world.

Tragically, the contemporary church often reflects a diluted form of Christianity, characterized by outward displays of religiosity but lacking authentic spiritual power. Rather than embodying the radical obedience and sacrificial love exemplified by Christ, many believers settle for a shallow form of faith that prioritizes comfort and convenience over costly discipleship.

In pursuing success and recognition, we may inadvertently build our towers of Babel—structures erected on the shaky foundations of human ambition rather than the solid rock of God's will. We measure our effectiveness by worldly metrics rather than the faithful stewardship of the gifts and resources entrusted to us by our Heavenly Father. Rather than living out God's purpose, which He pre-ordained for us, we live as echoes of the social media outlets and our family or religious indoctrinations.

Yet, amid the prevailing culture of spiritual complacency and compromise, a remnant of faithful disciples emerges—men and women who, like the early followers of Christ, embrace the call to radical obedience and sacrificial love. They recognize that true success in the Kingdom of God isn't measured by worldly standards but by faithfulness to our God-given purpose.

As we navigate the complexities of the contemporary Christian life, may we heed the call to surrender—yielding our lives unreservedly to the Lordship of Jesus Christ. In doing so, we become vessels through which God's glory is revealed, His kingdom is advanced, and His redemptive purposes are fulfilled.

The story of the rich, young ruler serves as a compelling invitation to examine the contents of our hearts and consider what indeed occupies the throne of our affections. Are we willing to surrender everything—our hopes, dreams, possessions, and ambitions—to follow Christ wholeheartedly? The journey of discipleship begins with a willingness to lay it all down at the feet of Jesus, trusting that He alone is worthy of our devotion and that His plans for us far surpass anything we could ever imagine.

Reflection Questions

What are the "riches" in your life that might be hindering your wholehearted devotion to Christ? How can you discern between healthy pursuits and those threatening to overshadow your commitment to Him?

How can we distinguish between superficial displays of religiosity and authentic spiritual power in today's church? What steps can we take to cultivate a deeper, more meaningful faith, prioritizing radical obedience and sacrificial love over mere outward appearances?

What areas do you resist or struggle with brokenness? How might embracing and surrendering to this process lead to more significant growth, healing, and fulfillment in your faith and personal development?

Chapter 3

What Are You After?

The pursuit of the American Dream has long been ingrained in the cultural ethos of the United States, often celebrated as a milestone of success and prosperity. However, for followers of Jesus in the U.S., the American Dream should not be the ultimate goal. Some individuals may live out this dream while simultaneously experiencing a spiritual nightmare. While material wealth and worldly success can certainly be part of an abundant life, they are not the primary reasons for Christ's sacrifice. Indeed, one can achieve success in the American sense through discipline, hard work, and favorable circumstances without necessarily acknowledging or depending on God.

Similarly, churches and ministries can be built without genuine dependence on God. Charismatic leaders with excellent public speaking skills and passionate delivery can draw crowds and foster a semblance of spirituality, even if their motives and methods are not rooted in genuine faith.

Throughout history, many cult leaders have demonstrated such traits without embodying actual submission to God.

True brokenness begins with recognizing that apart from being "born from above," the human heart is inherently wicked and deceitful. As the psalmist implored the reader in Psalm 139:23-24, genuine spiritual growth requires a willingness to confront and surrender our sinful inclinations:

> Search me [thoroughly], O God, and know my heart; Test me and know my anxious thoughts; And see if there is any wicked *or* hurtful way in me, And lead me in the everlasting way.

Despite these words, the notion of brokenness often evokes discomfort and resistance because it challenges our complacency with the status quo. When others share similar dysfunctions, we may unwittingly accept our shortcomings as the acceptable norm.

Yet, embracing brokenness is not an admission of defeat or a reflection of low self-esteem; instead, it acknowledges our need for transformation. It is bending both knees in submission to God's will, recognizing that our true identity and worth are found in Him alone. As Isaiah lamented his unworthiness in the presence of God's holiness, we, too, must humbly acknowledge our inadequacy apart from His grace: "Woe is me! For I am ruined, because I am a man of [ceremonially] unclean lips, and I live among a people of unclean lips; for my eyes have seen the King, the Lord of hosts" (Isaiah 6:5).

Brokenness is not merely about destruction

but about restoration and renewal. It is about allowing the Creator to mend and reshape His creation according to His perfect design. It involves falling on the Rock of Ages, yielding to the illuminating light of God's truth, and pleading for His unmerited favor. In this process, we understand that no good thing dwells within our flesh, and any semblance of righteousness is ultimately derived from God alone.

Reflection Questions

How does the concept of brokenness challenge your understanding of success and fulfillment in life?

In what areas of your life do you struggle to surrender to God's will and embrace His process of renewal and transformation?

What practical steps can you take today to embrace a mindset of abundance and generosity, recognizing the potential for growth and impact even amidst brokenness?

Chapter 4

A Different View of Holiness

An urgent call echoes from the heavenly realms for holiness among God's people. Throughout both the old and new Scriptures, abundant evidence underscores God's unwavering demand for holiness within His Church. Without holiness, Scripture declares, no one shall see the Lord. To grasp this divine imperative's significance, let us define holiness as the quality of being entirely separate from anything or anyone in the universe. Regarding God, holiness transcends mere actions or appearances; it is intrinsic to His nature. He is described as holy because He is unparalleled in every imaginable way. Even though the Scriptures describe Him as "like" certain things, nothing is comparable to Him.

Similarly, our pursuit of holiness necessitates separation from the ways of this world and a wholehearted consecration to the Master's will. It is not enough to distance ourselves from worldly influences; we must also dedicate ourselves entirely to God's purpose. While other religions may boast of their purity and separation, true holiness is not a product of human effort alone. Instead, it is the profound result of grace working within a life surrendered to the Master's touch.

In Jesus's hands, even the most ordinary elements—like bread—become vessels of holiness, transformed into instruments for miraculous provision. This transformation signifies more than just a physical change; it represents a consecration to the will of God where His divine purpose can be fully realized. As we yield ourselves to the Master's touch, allowing His grace to work within us, we become vessels through which His glory is revealed and His Kingdom is advanced.

This call to holiness extends far beyond individual piety; it encompasses the entirety of the Church. As the body of Christ, we are called to embody the holiness of our Lord, reflecting His purity and perfection to the world. Our collective pursuit of holiness is a testament to God's transformative power and a powerful witness to His redemptive work in the world.

The urgent call to holiness resounds in our day. It is a call to radical separation from the ways of this world and a wholehearted consecration to the will of God. As vessels of His grace and instruments of His purpose, may we embrace this call with humility and determination, allowing His holiness to permeate every aspect of our lives.

Reflection Questions

Reflecting on the definition of holiness as being entirely separate from anything or anyone in the universe, how does this understanding challenge your perception of God's nature and your pursuit of holiness?

How can you separate yourself from worldly influences and dedicate yourself more fully to God's purpose in your daily life?

Considering the transformation of ordinary elements into vessels of holiness in Jesus's hands, how can you surrender yourself more fully to the Master's touch to become a vessel through which His glory is revealed in your sphere of influence?

Chapter 5

Caution – May Contain Broken Pieces

In our journey through life, we confront a fundamental truth: We are all broken somehow. It's easy to overlook our brokenness when everything seems to be going well. Your life is sailing smoothly, relationships intact, and troubles seemingly nonexistent. In such moments, it's tempting to believe that because nothing feels broken, nothing truly is broken. But the reality is far more nuanced.

Brokenness isn't always accompanied by pain or apparent signs of distress. Some subtle brokenness lurks beneath the surface, unnoticed until circumstances reveal its presence. Moreover, our perception of brokenness can be distorted by the brokenness of those around us. When everyone else struggles, it's easy to conclude that our struggles aren't significant. But comparing ourselves to others is a flawed metric. The Apostle Paul warned against this in his writings, urging us to measure ourselves against the perfect standard of Christ rather than the flawed standards of humanity:

> We do not have the audacity to put ourselves in the same class or compare ourselves with some who [supply testimonials to] commend themselves. When they measure themselves by themselves and compare themselves with themselves, they lack wisdom and behave like fools. We, on the other hand, will not boast beyond our proper limit, but [will keep] within the limits of our commission (territory, authority) which God has granted to us as a measure, which reaches and includes even you (2 Corinthians 10:12-13).

The root cause of our brokenness is sin. Regardless of the specific sins we've committed, the overarching truth is that sin has fractured our relationship with God and distorted His original design for our lives. Like bread dough kneaded by a baker, our lives are shaped by the sins we've committed and the sins committed against us, forming a complex tapestry of brokenness.

Yet, amid the brokenness, there is hope. Just as the baker places the bread dough in the oven to be transformed into something new, so too does Jesus take our broken lives and work to reshape them according to His divine plan. It's a process of breaking open and breaking off the things that have become ingrained in our character, restoring us to wholeness.

But the journey to wholeness begins with humility and self-awareness. We must acknowledge our brokenness and invite the Holy Spirit to illuminate areas of darkness within us. The psalmist's plea, "Search me, O God, and know my heart! Try me and know my thoughts!" (Psalm 139:23), becomes our cry for divine intervention.

Without the light of the Holy Spirit, we risk remaining blinded by our ignorance, unaware of the depths of our brokenness. It's a sobering realization that opens the door to healing and restoration. As we humble ourselves before God, inviting His searching gaze into the recesses of our souls, we position ourselves to receive His mercy and grace.

So, let us not shy away from the broken pieces within us but instead offer them up to the Master Potter, trusting in His ability to reshape and renew us. May we embrace the journey of brokenness as a pathway to wholeness, allowing God to transform our broken lives into vessels of His glory.

Our brokenness is not a sign of failure but an opportunity for redemption. It reminds us that we are in desperate need of God's grace and mercy. As we surrender our brokenness to Him, He promises to heal and restore us, transforming our lives into beautiful testimonies of His love and power.

Reflection Questions

How does our perception of brokenness influence our understanding of God's redemptive work?

How can we cultivate humility and self-awareness to more fully embrace the process of transformation and restoration in Christ?

How can we support and encourage others experiencing brokenness, reflecting Christ's love and compassion in their journey towards healing and restoration?

Chapter 6

Nothing Broken, Nothing Missing

A life surrendered to the loving hands of the Master undergoes a profound transformation—a transformation that leads to wholeness and completeness. In our journey with God, the concept of peace, often translated from the Hebrew word "shalom," takes on a deeper meaning than a mere absence of conflict. While many may long for quiet and serenity amidst life's chaos, true biblical peace encompasses more than external tranquility.

Shalom signifies a state of completeness, soundness, and well-being in every aspect of life. It encompasses physical health, emotional stability, relational harmony, and spiritual vitality. It embodies a sense of wholeness and contentment that transcends external circumstances, rooted in a deep-seated trust in the person of Jesus Christ.

When we allow ourselves to be broken by the hands of God, it is not a process of destruction but one of divine reconstruction. While the world may associate breaking with devastation, God's intention is always redemption, restoration, and renewal. As the Apostle John reminds us, the enemy seeks to steal, kill, and destroy, but Jesus came to give us abundant life—an abundant life marked by the fullness of God's shalom.

In the hands of the Master, brokenness becomes a gateway to restoration and healing. Through our life's brokenness, God works to remove the barriers that hinder His shalom from permeating every area of our existence. Just as a potter molds and shapes clay to form a vessel of beauty and purpose, God shapes and molds us through brokenness to become vessels of His peace and wholeness in the world.

As we surrender to God's transformative work within us, we discover that true shalom is not dependent on external circumstances but flows from an intimate relationship with the Prince of Peace. It is a peace that surpasses understanding, guarding our hearts and minds in Christ Jesus, even amid life's storms and struggles.

Without the touch of God upon our hip socket, we will continue unchanged. As Jacob wrestled with the Lord's Angel all night for the blessing, we must be just as willing and determined (see Genesis 32:24). Just as Jacob's name was changed to Israel after the wrestling match, we too must allow the hand of the Almighty to make whatever character changes He deems necessary for our destiny. As you may recall, Jacob was a trickster and swindler before the angelic encounter, but afterward, with a corresponding name change, he became the Prince of God. May our intentions, our contending with God, yield such a noble outcome.

Jacob fought for a blessing, though I don't think he thought the blessing would come with a life-altering touch in his body. The Scriptures are silent as to the specific blessing Jacob sought, but I believe he agreed with the old song, "Any way He blesses me, I'll be satisfied." Asking God for the blessing is one thing; receiving the blessing is something entirely different. To receive the manifestation of the blessing of God requires first a breaking. The blessing for Jacob wasn't the hip socket issue. The fact that his leg was now "deformed" was proof that God had touched him.

I don't know what that deformity looked like, but I can believe that it changed the way or how Jacob turned Israel and walked the rest of His life. The breaking isn't the blessing, nor does the blessing stop or cancel the blessing. Instead, the breaking qualifies us for the release of profound blessing. The manifestation of the blessing follows the breaking; the breaking releases the blessing.

Many come to church to be blessed. Often parents, even those who don't belong to a particular church or haven't attended church in years, seek the blessing of the Church once they have a baby in their life. That's an important thing to do. They may not be walking with the Lord themselves, but they recognize a life with a blessing is better than one without one. After all, who doesn't want to be blessed? The problem arises when we realize that the blessing requires something on our part.

As I mentioned in an earlier chapter, the rich young ruler who wanted to follow Jesus until Jesus asked him to sell all he had and give it to the poor is a classic example of wanting something without personal sacrifice. Many of us, probably most of us, have faced the reality that going further in life requires changes. For instance, if you want better health, it will require significant changes to your diet, exercise, sleep, relationships, etc. If you don't make substantial changes, you won't have the health God has decreed, which is yours. Some say they want to own their own business, but when faced with the reality of the sacrifice they will have to make, the savings, the education—the credit repair, and so on, many say, "No, I don't want a business."

Reflection Questions

How does the concept of brokenness challenge our traditional understanding of peace and completeness in life, particularly in the context of biblical shalom?

Reflecting on the narrative of Jacob's wrestling with the Angel of the Lord, how can we cultivate a similar determination and willingness to contend with God for transformation and blessing in our own lives?

In what ways do we often seek God's blessings without fully understanding or embracing the process of breaking and transformation that precedes their manifestation? How can we develop a more profound willingness to undergo the necessary changes for God's blessings to be fully realized?

Chapter 7

The Cost of Blessing

We often desire the blessing without fully comprehending the cost associated with it. The blessing is not just a gift bestowed upon us; it's an invitation to participate in God's divine plan for our lives. It requires us to align our will with His, to surrender our desires and ambitions to the One who knows us best. Like Jacob, we must be willing to wrestle with God and contend for His blessings, even if it means enduring discomfort or facing uncertainty.

Moreover, the blessing is often preceded by a breaking—a moment of profound transformation where our old selves are stripped away, and we are made new in Christ. Just as Jacob limped away from his encounter with God, forever changed but blessed beyond measure, so too we must be willing to embrace the breaking process, knowing it is the pathway to true blessing and fulfillment in God's kingdom.

Let us neither avoid the wrestling match with

God nor recoil from the breaking process that precedes the blessing. Instead, let us lean into the discomfort, trusting that God's hand is at work in our lives, shaping us into vessels fit for His purposes. May we, like Jacob, emerge from the struggle with a new identity, a renewed purpose, and a profound sense of God's blessing upon our lives.

Reflection Questions

How does our understanding of the cost of blessing shape our willingness to pursue God's divine plan for our lives, even when it requires discomfort or uncertainty?

Reflecting on Jacob's wrestling with God and the subsequent breaking process, what aspects of our old selves do we need to surrender to embrace God's transformative work in our lives fully?

How can we cultivate a posture of trust and surrender during seasons of wrestling and breaking, recognizing that they are essential steps toward experiencing the fullness of God's blessings and fulfillment in our lives?

Chapter 8

The Necessity of Obedience

The pursuit of God's blessing necessitates obedience. While it's indisputable that God has already blessed us, to experience more of His blessings requires our willingness to align our lives with His will. Unfortunately, some succumb to the deception of desiring blessing while disobeying God's commands. God's grace positions us for immeasurable blessing, but obedience puts us in the direct path to receive the manifestations. Regrettably, many in the church crave instant gratification, expecting rewards without putting in effort or obedience.

This entitlement mentality pervades various aspects of our lives. We want success, wealth, and comfort without putting in the hard work or making the required sacrifices. Instead of preparing ourselves diligently, we expect blessings to be handed to us on a silver platter. This attitude reflects a profound sense of entitlement and ingratitude, maintaining that we deserve the blessing apart from obeying the word of God.

However, the reality is that true blessings come to those who are willing to be broken before God. This brokenness involves surrendering our ways, habits, and desires at the altar of obedience. It requires acknowledging our shortcomings and being willing to undergo a transformative process under God's guidance.

In essence, true blessings are not bestowed upon the entitled or the complacent but upon those who humbly submit themselves to God's will and undergo the refining process of brokenness. As we yield ourselves to God's transformative work, we position ourselves to receive the fullness of His blessings and experience His divine perfection in our lives.

Consider the production of olive oil, a substance frequently mentioned in the Bible as a symbol of blessing and anointing. It takes approximately 333 olives to make just one gallon of olive oil. This remarkable statistic carries significant symbolism, as the number three holds profound significance in the Bible, representing the Trinity—God the Father, God the Son, and God the Holy Spirit. It symbolizes divine perfection and completeness.

Olive oil is renowned for its medicinal and therapeutic properties and has been a staple in Middle Eastern cultures for millennia. Its multifaceted utility, from skin ointment to culinary ingredients to symbols of spiritual anointing, underscores its significance in ancient societies. Olives must undergo a rigorous crushing and pressing process to obtain olive oil. Despite the labor-intensive nature of the process, the resulting oil is highly valued for its purity and potency.

Similarly, our lives are akin to olives awaiting transformation. Just as olives must undergo crushing to yield oil, we, too, must experience a process of breaking and refinement to unleash our true potential. This "breaking" process is not easy—it requires us to confront our weaknesses, insecurities, and limitations head-on. Yet, through this process, our most valuable qualities are liberated and refined.

The olive oil extraction process analogy resonates deeply with a believer's spiritual journey. The Apostle Paul's words in 2 Corinthians 4:7 remind us that we carry a treasure within us, but it's housed in earthen vessels—our imperfect, flawed selves:

> But we have this precious treasure [the good news about salvation] in [unworthy] earthen vessels [of human frailty], so that the grandeur and surpassing greatness of the power will be [shown to be] from God [His sufficiency] and not from ourselves.

However, it's precisely through our brokenness that the glory and power of God are most clearly revealed. Just as the olive oil, we must undergo trials and tribulations to reveal the divine treasure within us.

The ultimate example of this transformative process is found in the life and death of Jesus Christ. Despite His divine nature, Jesus willingly submitted to the agony of the cross, enduring unimaginable suffering and humiliation. His flesh, though marred and broken, contained the most precious substance—the atoning blood that would wash away humanity's sins. Jesus brought deliverance and redemption to all who would believe in Him through His sacrificial death and resurrection.

Jesus' crushing symbolizes the profound truth that our most significant victories often emerge from our deepest struggles—the profound image of Jesus in a garden of olive trees. As we embrace the breaking process and yield ourselves to the transformative power of God, we discover that our greatest strength lies in our surrender to His will. Therefore, let us not shrink from the trials and challenges that come our way but rather embrace them as opportunities for growth and transformation.

Reflection Questions

Reflecting on the olive oil extraction process analogy, what areas of your life are currently undergoing a "breaking" or refining process? How do you perceive these challenges contributing to your growth and transformation?

Consider embracing brokenness as a pathway to wholeness and spiritual maturity. How can you cultivate a surrender mindset and openness to God's transformative work? How might this perspective shift influence your approach to challenges and difficulties?

Reflecting on the concept of God's blessings being preceded by a breaking process, what blessings or transformations have you experienced in your life that followed a period of difficulty or struggle? How do these experiences shape your understanding of God's faithfulness and redemptive work?

Chapter 9

The Garden of Gethsemane – The Place of Breaking

Where and when did Jesus die? I realize that the Scripture speaks of Jesus dying on the cross on Golgotha's hill. That is where He "gave up the Ghost" and breathed His last. However, an experience in the Garden of Gethsemane made death on the cross possible. First, the garden was not a flower or vegetable garden but an olive tree grove and olive press. This is where tons of olives were crushed for thousands of years to produce olive oil. Jesus often went there to pray (John 18:2). It was the place where He communed with His Father.

And that night, His final night, He went to the garden to pray and invited His disciples to accompany Him. As the night progressed, He found His disciples sleeping rather than praying. He approached them two times and found them fast asleep. His darkest hour turned out to be His most lonely hour. The "breaking" that releases the treasure occurs when we allow our will and ways to fall lifeless to the ground, crushed under the weight of His sovereignty.

The Gospel writer remarks that as Jesus wrestled with the will of His Father, He sweated drops of blood. The pressure was so profound, the pain in the immediate future so great, that He bled through His pores. But because of His view of the tomorrow, He endured the painful present for the joy set before Him. He endured the cross, despising the shame (Hebrew 12:2).

Jesus asked for this cup to pass without drinking it. The cup was the cup of redemption, representing His blood. It was the fact He would have to die the death on the cross and bear the sins of the entire universe—past, present, and future—He would become sin personified. It was a weight that was incomprehensible. His prayer throughout the night centered around a plea, "If this cup could pass." His response was nevertheless "not my will." This, I contend, is where Jesus died.

In His resignation to the will of His Father over His will and desire, that was the point of breaking. I firmly believe that if Jesus had not had this moment of embracing the will of God in prayer, He would not have been able to do the most sacrificial act of all time, which was to die for an entire world. He became our Savior and our Substitute.

The work our Heavenly Father has for us to do on the earth will not and cannot be accomplished without experiencing our own personal Gethsemanes. The "olives" and "grapes" of our lives must first be crushed before the precious life flow will be released to bring healing and deliverance to the world around us. I will address this topic again later.

Jesus took the bread, blessed it, broke it, and gave the fragments to the disciples to be distributed in a picture of our life. He will take the broken, fragmented pieces of your life and share them with a hungry world desperately needing what you consider leftovers. Hungry people aren't interested in the beauty of the loaf. They're fixated on their stomachs being satisfied. You can feed them if and only after you are broken.

Reflection Questions

Reflecting on Jesus's experience in the Garden of Gethsemane, consider moments when you wrestle with God's will versus your desires. How did these moments shape your understanding of surrender and sacrifice?

Contemplate the significance of Jesus's prayer in Gethsemane as a model for our prayer life. How can we emulate Jesus's posture of submission and trust in our prayers, particularly during times of difficulty and uncertainty?

Consider the metaphor of the olive press in the Garden of Gethsemane as a symbol of the breaking process in our lives. In what ways have you experienced moments of breaking or crushing that ultimately led to spiritual growth and transformation?

Chapter 10

An Intimate Encounter

To be blessed is a desire of all people everywhere. Somehow, we know that a blessing is good, and curses are bad. Whether we are religious or not, we would rather have a blessing than a curse. Often, people come to Churches to be blessed. They believe that as God's servant, if I speak a word about their life, a good word, their life will be better. I think that to be biblical, but that's not the whole story of what it means to be blessed. Death and life reside in your mouth, too, not just in your mind: "Death and life are in the power of the tongue" (Proverbs 18:21). If you speak curses over your life and situations, that's what's coming your way. You must learn to watch our speech, for your words have inherent power.

When we think of someone blessing their food before consuming it, we call it a blessing. Or if someone sneezes, we say, "God bless you." Or, as it reads in other examples of Jesus feeding multitudes, the word "blessing" refers to giving thanks. However, in Mark 6:41, Jesus did not use the Greek word for thanksgiving or eucharist, but instead, He used the word *eulogy*:

> Taking the five loaves and two fish, He looked up to heaven and said a blessing [of praise and thanksgiving to the Father]. Then He broke the loaves and [repeatedly] gave them to the disciples to set before the people; and He divided up the two fish among them all.

A eulogy is often given at the funeral service of a deceased person, so it's noteworthy that Jesus chose this word to speak over a loaf of bread!

When Jesus "blessed" the bread, He eulogized it. He spoke a good word about the bread's future. He declared what He heard from heaven into the bread. Jesus received the Father's mind regarding the potential of the bread. You are no different. Instead of waiting for a eulogy to be delivered over your corpse, Jesus has declared good things for you now. The Bible teaches you that God has already chosen works you should do (Ephesians 2:10). And despite the breaking after the blessing, you remain blessed, for the breaking releases the blessing contained within it.

Contrary to what some think, being broken doesn't disqualify us from the blessing, it positions us for its manifestation. We often forget the blessings in the difficult season of life or during the breaking periods. We forget that before we begin "life," God has already eulogized us. He has a plan for us that includes an abundant life. We must never forget in the dark what we heard in the light; in light of His eulogy

Reflection Questions

Reflecting on the concept of blessing as portrayed in this chapter, consider how your words and declarations shape your reality. How can you align your speech with God's promises and eulogize your circumstances with positive, life-giving declarations? How might a shift in your language positively impact your outlook and experiences?

Explore the significance of Jesus' use of the word "eulogy" in blessing the bread, indicating a declaration of good things for its future. How does this perspective challenge your understanding of God's intentions for your life?

Contemplate the relationship between blessing and brokenness highlighted in this chapter. How does the revelation that breaks and releases the blessing within reshape your perspective on adversity and challenges?

Chapter 11

The Best Part Is

On the Inside Of You

A woman came with an alabaster vial of very costly and precious perfume of pure nard; and she broke the vial and poured the perfume over His head. – Mark 14:3

This account of a woman who crashed a dinner party where Jesus was attending is another profound example of what happens when something breaks. Upon seeing Jesus, she broke the box or the seal for that contained within it to be released. I'm sure this costly perfume was preserved in an ornate or decorative box. It probably sat in a prominent place as a memorial of happier times, or maybe it was part of her dowry. Although everyone could see the box's outer beauty, the inner contents were of greater value.

Much conjecture exists regarding where this woman, a notorious sinner, got this expensive gift. Was this her dowry to be presented to her future husband's family upon marriage? Is this a gift from her male friends or purchased with the money she earned by laying on her back trying to be loved? We don't know. History is silent. But for our discussion, this "gift "represents what is resident in all of us. There is something within us, placed there by the blessing of God, that will never be released until there is a breaking—a voluntary breaking of humanity.

But who likes to be broken? No one. However, the truth is life can be full of opportunities for brokenness. It's not the tragedies or the consequences of our sins that I'm referring to, but rather when we lay down our lives in and for Christ is the breaking process.

Taking what we think is valuable and laying it down, with no strings attached at the feet of Jesus, is when the blessing is released. The Scripture tells us this woman heard that Jesus was at a particular house at a specific time. The guests of Simon, whose house Jesus was reclining at, questioned the master's credibility for being so friendly with "this woman." To make matters worse, it was the treasurer of Jesus' ministry, Judas, who criticized such a wasteful gesture.

Among the many lessons that this nameless woman teaches us is that, when it comes to giving to the Master, no amount or sacrifice is too much. There will be some who say you have gone too far in your devotion. They will say you don't need to do all that. Let them talk. Let them have their opinion because it doesn't matter what they say unless you let it matter. Your giving of yourself is what qualifies you for the blessing of God. It's the demonstration of your "all in" rather than some religious tipping of God that registers in heaven.

This is a relevant word for those with means or even riches. You may think you are all in because you give much (most wealthy in the church world do not give sacrificially, but out of their abundance). But God doesn't want or need your money. He's looking for and at your heart. The Apostle Paul remarked to the church in Macedonia that "they first gave themselves to the Lord and then to us" (2 Corinthian 8:5). What God has always desired was our conscious, intentional yielding of our heart and will to Him. It is by our surrender that we most honor the sacrifice Jesus made for us.

Reflection Questions

Reflecting on the woman's story with the costly perfume, consider your valuable gifts or talents that remain hidden or underutilized. How can you break the "box" or barriers that prevent these gifts from being released and used for God's glory?

Explore the significance of the woman's extravagant devotion in pouring out the costly perfume on Jesus. How does her sacrificial giving challenge your understanding of generosity and devotion to Christ?

Contemplate the role of sacrifice and surrender in experiencing the fullness of God's blessing in your life. How does giving yourself wholly to the Lord precede receiving His abundant blessings?

Chapter 12

Broken is Better

The adage "less is more" is an oxymoron. How can something that is diminished accomplish more? The answer to this is found in the miracle of a seed. A seed is a deceptive little thing, for though small, it contains the DNA of an entire organism. For instance, an acorn, the seed of an oak tree, possesses a mighty, majestic living thing within its tiny body.

However, no one could know that just by looking at its outer shell. If you cut it open, you still wouldn't see the vastness of its potential. But place this little acorn in the right environment, allow it to suffer decay in the dark, cold dampness of the earth, and from it will emerge not just a tree but an infinite number of trees.

You may be able to count the number of acorns on a tree, but you can't know how many trees are in one acorn. It is the same with us as with an acorn or any other seed. Our Creator pre-pro grammed us with infinite potential. Tragically, most folks die without ever seeing any of their divine destiny realized, for which there are several reasons. One of the most important is our unwillingness to submit our lives into the hands of the Master. Only by dying to one's self and agenda positions us for the grand release.

The fact that Jesus gave what was broken to His disciples for distribution is revealing. As I stated in the previous chapter, He only provides what is broken. But as it relates to us, when we see ourselves in a broken position or, should I say condition, we question our potential and capability. We felt more potent and more assured when we were all together. We had more confidence in accomplishing or overcoming the challenges before us.

But then Jesus' words speak to us: "Apart from Me, you can do nothing." Our strength, ability, and wisdom fail in the face of our life issues. It's not until we are in pieces at His hands that we are positioned for our most significant moments. Please note, however, that I wrote "in pieces at His Hands." Some, especially the religious, are educated yet ignorant of the will of God in this area. It's often taught that the greater the personal tragedy, the deeper the relationship with the Lord. That sickness, disease, death of loved ones, and abuses of all kinds are the "breaking and testing" of God. Only in those is God somehow teaching us the lessons we need. Only after those will be closer to the Lord.

However, it's been my experience that those horrible events make people bitter, not better. They question God's love and the purpose of Christ. The Church of the Lord Jesus Christ has preached this fallacy and consequently, many blame God for what the devil has done. The brokenness I'm referring to that produces lasting impact is a brokenness that comes from the revelation of who Christ is and what He has done for you. When you see Him and experience His love, regardless of your status in life, you are broken. You become painfully but gloriously aware of His holiness and your inadequacies, insecurities, pride, sin, and selfishness.

You see, in no uncertain terms, your limits in the face of His limitlessness. Your utter helplessness, apart from His grace and strength, becomes evident. But rather than this being a depressing moment, you realize that His ability is now your ability, that you are, at best, a conduit through which His awe-inspiring love and unbridled power can flow.

Jesus essentially gave you back to us. In essence, He says, "Now that I have broken you, you are fit to serve My people." At that moment, you realize your weakness magnifies His strength. And then you see how it's possible to become more by becoming less. What an awesome God we serve!

Reflection Questions

Reflecting on the analogy of the seed's growth potential, consider the hidden potential within yourself that may have yet to be realized. In what areas of your life do you sense untapped potential or unfulfilled destiny?

Explore the concept of brokenness as a prerequisite for divine empowerment and effectiveness in serving others. How does embracing brokenness lead to a deeper reliance on God's strength rather than one's own abilities?

Contemplate the transformative power of encountering Christ's love and grace in brokenness. How does recognizing your limitations and inadequacies in light of God's holiness lead to a more profound dependence on Him?

Chapter 13

One Look Can Change Your Life

After Jesus commanded the crowd to sit down in a particular order, He took the bread and looked up to heaven. This text has powerful imagery we must not overlook in our haste to get to the "miracle." I submit that if Jesus had not looked up to heaven before blessing the bread and the fish, there would not have been a supernatural answer to the people's hunger. The bread would have remained an average, ordinary barley loaf—the staple meal of the poor. Heaven still has your answer.

Why did the Son of God, the very Creator of all things, need to be looking up to heaven? After all, He is the Word who made everything. Why was He looking up to heaven? There's a two-part answer to this question. First, it's because heaven has our answer. Heaven is the very picture of what should be in our lives. Remember Jesus teaching His disciples to pray, "... thy will be done on earth as it is in heaven" (Matthew 6:10, KJV)? I sense that Jesus needed to know the Father's perspective regarding that situation. Heaven's perspective is always the right perspective.

By looking up, Jesus acknowledged the Living God as His answer, His source for all things. The psalmist David said, "I will look unto the hills from whence cometh my help, my help cometh from the Lord who has made heaven and earth" (Psalm 121:1-2). This is an important aspect of prayer. Prayer to God isn't just talking and seeing and hearing God's perspective. He takes the bread and fish and "looks up to heaven." Practically speaking, take your life—it may appear to you to be typical, average, uninspiring, routine, mundane—but now look up to Heaven. What is the God of the Heavens saying about your situation and life?

The second reason Jesus looked into the heavens prior to breaking and blessing the bread is to get a specific "word" for that specific situation. The phrase "to look up to heaven" literally means to "peer into the seat of order eternal." In other words, Jesus looked into the abode of God for the perfect image of what everything should be like, what would become of the bread. This is where we too should get our blueprint for our life and the situations perplexing us. His looking up was no mere head movement, but rather it was the acquiring heaven's will for the bread and the feeding of thousands of people.

Reflection Questions

How does looking up to heaven before performing a miracle symbolize our need to align with God's perspective and divine order? What practical steps can we take to seek God's perspective and guidance in our daily challenges and decisions?

Reflecting on Jesus' action of looking up to heaven, consider how it underscores the importance of acknowledging God as our ultimate source and provider. How can cultivating a mindset of dependency on God's wisdom and provision enhance our faith journey and empower us to confidently face life's uncertainties?

Looking up to heaven implies seeking a higher perspective beyond our earthly circumstances. How can we apply this principle in our approach to prayer and problem solving, particularly when faced with challenges or limitations?

Chapter 14

Imitate To Replicate

The Son of God only did what He saw the Father do. He only said what He heard the Father say. All His movements were mirror images of the Father in heaven. So why would we expect this moment to be any different for us? He checked in with heaven by looking up. He acknowledged that He would only move at the direction of the God Most High. Not even our Savior moved apart from the Father (see John 5:19).

I want to draw your attention to the word *heaven*. The Scripture says Jesus looked up to heaven, not meaning just at the sky. The word *heaven* in this verse means "the vaulted expanse of the sky with all things visible in it, the seat of order of things eternal and consummately perfect; where God dwells and other heavenly beings" (www.BlueLetterBible.com, copyright 2008-2012, Zetetec LLC).

When Jesus looked up, He was looking unto someone, not just changing His gaze. He first looked at the bread that was given to Him. He looked away from its natural ingredients to the Creator and

Sustainer of all things to get heaven's perspective of what He held in His hand. He took his attention away from the familiar to gain insight from the heavenly One.

For you to emulate Jesus in order to receive the miraculous, you must break your fixation on what can be seen and look unto the heavens. After all, you are seated in the heavens with Christ and in Christ. You are not really of this world. You live on the earth, in the world, but you are not of this world. This is the challenge. Let's pause here for a minute.

Being born-again means, in part, that you are a partaker of the divine nature (see 1 Peter 1:24). You were born-again by an incorruptible seed—divine sperm, if you will. And the moment when you confessed Jesus Christ as your Lord, receiving Him as your Savior and Substitute, you were placed in Him. The God of the heavens, Jehovah, as well as Satan and demons, know this. The problem is *we* don't know this or live like it if we do.

You were translated out of the dominion and slavery of Satan and put into the family of God by blood. You are now in the Kingdom of God and the Son, a blood-type change. You experienced a spiritual DNA change. So when He was crucified, you were being crucified too. When He died, you died too. You also rose out of the grave when He arose from the dead. When He ascended to the heavens to sit on the Father's right hand, you ascended and sat down at the Father's right hand too. He raised you far above all principality and power—above sickness, above depression, above addiction, above poverty, above lack, above the basic elements of this life. Even death is your servant. Claim your divine rights as a child of God.

Reflection Questions

How does imitating Jesus' actions, particularly in seeking direction from the Father, challenge your usual approach to decision making and problem-solving?

Reflect on a recent situation where you faced a challenge or need. Did you first rely on your understanding or immediately seek guidance from a higher power?

Consider that being born-again means participating in the divine nature and being seated with Christ in the heavens. How does this perspective shift your understanding of your identity and authority as a believer?

Chapter 15

Look Up If You Want Heaven to Come Down

Taking the five loaves and two fish, He looked up to heaven and said a blessing [of praise and thanksgiving to the Father]. Then He broke the loaves and [repeatedly] gave them to the disciples to set before the people; and He divided up the two fish among them all. – Mark 6:41

The usage of the phrase "he looked up" in Mark 6:41 means to recover lost sight, not merely to gaze up to the ceiling. The Greek word is *anableps* and it means "to look up or to recover (lost) sight" (www.BlueLetterBible.com, copyright 2008-2012,

Zetetec LLC). What does this tell you? Whatever you are facing right now, if you continually look at the situation without looking to "heaven," you will remain blind, or at least blind to God's thoughts about it.

When Jesus looked unto heaven, He looked into the "seat of order eternal." He looked into consummate perfection, the literal dwelling place of God and other heavenly beings. A stronger form of this word is found in Acts 7:55. Stephen, a deacon in the Lord's church and filled with the Holy Ghost, was being stoned to death. The Bible says, "But he, being full of the Holy Ghost, looked up steadfastly into heaven, and saw the glory of God, and Jesus standing on the right hand of God" (Acts 7:55, KJV). This is the only account in which Jesus is seen standing rather than sitting at the right hand of God. I believe Jesus was giving Stephen a standing ovation for staying true to His testimony in the face of certain death.

But the word used for looking up in this verse means "to fix one's gaze, unbroken concentration." When you are being tested and tried because of your stand for Jesus, you must have an "unbreakable gaze into the heavens," which will allow you to recover your sight. A teacher stated that the number one reason people fail is broken focus. Stay focused on the right One and the right Thing. Oh, how necessary is it for us to have Dad's eternal perspective on our temporary problems! Having a supernatural viewpoint on a natural situation is one of the main benefits of prayer.

Jesus did not speak a curse over the bread or the fish. He said a blessing over them, a eulogy, as I mentioned earlier. When He looked up into heaven,

He recovered His sight and perspective about the potential of the bread and fish. When you continually speak about the past as if it's now, you are cursing your today and sentencing your tomorrow to be the same as your past. For instance, if Jesus spoke to the loaf of bread and said, "You are only bread; you can only make 22 sandwiches." You definitely can't meet any challenge like this by cursing or speaking negatively. Some would say this would simply be telling the truth, calling it like it is. Yes, but what it is different from what it can be!

Reflection Questions

Reflect on a recent situation when you faced a challenge or difficulty. Did you find yourself fixating on the problem itself, or could you focus on seeking guidance from a higher perspective?

Consider "recovering sight" by looking to heaven in moments of trial or difficulty. How might this practice of seeking a higher perspective shift your mindset and approach to challenges in your life?

Consider the power of words and perspective in shaping outcomes. Have you ever found yourself speaking negatively about a situation, essentially "cursing" your present and future by dwelling on the past?

Chapter 16

Closer To Home

When you look at your life—the mess ups, the wrecks, the disappointments, the divorce, the sin, the poor judgment, the lack, the inadequacy, the failed attempts at business, marriage, relationships or even living for God—if you're not careful, you conclude, "I am what I am and this is all that I am." Your past doesn't have to be your tomorrow. So, prophesy to yourself. Prophesy to your body. Prophesy to your money, family, and children. Stop talking about what is obvious. Call into existence those things that do not yet exist in your world, rather than focusing on things as they presently are. This can only be done as you look unto the seat of order of the eternal—looking up to the heavens.

You might be saying to yourself, *I'm nothing more than a thief, liar, murderer, hypocrite, whoremonger, alcoholic, selfish mother, and an absentee father, drug addict, and demonized hellion. Lazy, jealous, gossiper, and bona fide witch. Homosexual, faithless, unbeliever.* You have a position within your church but are not living up to any measure of it.

You might be remembering how you had sex with this one and that one, how you hurt your kids, abused your husband or your wife, robbed your grandparents, abandoned your responsibilities, lost your home, gambled away your future, abused others, and have been abused by others. I'm talking about the negative self-talk that far too many Christians participate in.

The difference is that you are the bread that God has blessed, but right now, you see yourself only as what has happened to you and what you have done. You're still looking at yourself rather than looking up to Jesus and what He has done for and in you. Many still feel unlovable because some foolish people failed to see their value. You still see yourself as the one who got left at the altar, who isn't worthy of being loved. You're still looking in the wrong direction, with the wrong set of eyes. Get your eyes off the unblessed, unbroken bread.

You will now say, *I am fearfully and wonderfully made. I am the apple of His eye, the righteousness of God in Christ. I'm a new person in Christ. I'm seated in heavenly places, sitting in the company and conversation of the Godhead. I'm the dwelling place and temple of the Holy Spirit. I have God's wisdom and the peace of God. I'm the healed of God. I have the power of God, and the living Christ works with and through me.*

This is where it has to get real for you. This is when you are genuinely challenged to change your life based on your view from heaven. What is your life based on? Upon an ordinary view or perspective? What would happen if you had an audience with the God of heaven and earth, and asked Him, "What do You see in me? What is it that You want me to do and become?" And based on His responses, you act with all deliberate speed on that new information. What would your life look like within a year? How do you think you would feel?

Take your Bible, get alone, and look up to heaven by looking down into God's Word. I'm not expecting you to look up literally into the heavens. But through quiet, devotional reading, meditation on the Word, and talking to your Heavenly Father and listening for Him talking to you, you will gain heaven's perspective and heaven's will. And then speak to only what you see and hear from the Word. By doing so, you will bring heaven into your everyday bread and all too familiar life.

You have clouds blocking your view of the Son. You have been through some storms and are so used to listening to the weather report—a form of prophecy, by the way—that you live your life based on past knowledge and experiences. See Jesus. Allow God to bring heaven's life to you and manifest through you. Speak heaven. Speak heaven. Speak heaven.

Reflection Questions

Reflect on your self-talk and the narratives you speak over your life. Have you found yourself dwelling on past mistakes and shortcomings, defining yourself by them? How might embracing a perspective of prophecy and speaking into existence what you desire to see change how you view yourself and your potential?

Consider the contrast between seeing yourself solely through your own eyes versus seeing yourself through how Jesus sees you. How might shifting your perspective from self-condemnation to acceptance and love transform your daily life and interactions?

Imagine if you were to align your actions and words solely with what you see and hear from heaven. How might this change how you approach challenges, relationships, and goals?

Chapter 17

Heavenly Perspective and Fragments of Grace

Yet another example of Jesus looking up is found in Mark 7. There we read about a young girl, deaf and dumb, meaning she couldn't speak or hear. Jesus put his fingers in her ears, looked up into heaven, sighed, and commanded her ears to open. Before Jesus performed that miracle, He first got a heavenly perspective. He looked into the heart of His Father, and saw how things ought to be, not what things used to be.

The view of heaven was that her body was perfect in every way—speaking, hearing, walking, talking, laughing, singing. So Jesus, once He got the heavenly perspective, said and did what heaven showed Him. The deaf girl heard, and the mute girl spoke. This is the expressed will of God—hearing, seeing, and then doing heaven on earth. Pray heavenly prayers. Do heavenly actions. Think heavenly thoughts. What did Jesus teach His disciples to pray" "Our Father, who art in heaven, hallowed by thy name, thy Kingdom come, thy will be done, on *earth* as it is in *heaven*!"

As we conclude our story of usefulness through brokenness, the fragments, the broken pieces of bread that feed the multitude, the same is true for you. Your brokenness releases the precious treasure of God's grace to the hurting and the helpless. While experiencing brokenness is nothing to be excited about at first thought, the result will be that you can give what they need rather than what you think they need. Brokenness takes you out of your limited mindsets based on your natural abilities and gifting. The real, lasting blessing for others will only come through as you come to the end of yourself. It is at that point that God's goodness is revealed.

Brokenness creates a reliance on the work of grace in your life. Brokenness provides the best opportunity to allow Jesus to be glorified. "Such as I have, I give unto thee" were words uttered from the mouth of the Apostle Peter who, through a personal revelation, realized that all he had to offer was what was left over after he had been exposed as a coward. All that you have and ever hope to be, you owe it all to His amazing grace.

Reflection Questions

Reflect on Jesus healing the deaf and mute girl in Mark 7. How does Jesus's looking up to heaven before performing the miracle challenge your perspective on prayer and action?

Consider the concept of brokenness as a pathway to usefulness and grace. Have you experienced moments of brokenness in your life? How did these experiences shape your understanding of God's grace and your ability to minister to others?

Reflect on the phrase "such as I have, I give unto thee." How does this statement resonate with your journey of brokenness and reliance on God's grace?

Chapter 18

Distribution of Brokenness And Embracing Inadequacy

When Jesus finished breaking the bread, he distributed the broken pieces to the disciples who became the distributors. Perhaps these distributors had not believed Jesus when He told them to feed 5,000 men with fragments from only five loaves. But it is only in the obedience—in the doing of what Jesus says—that miracles are to be found. Then, with fragments of bread in their hands, they approached this orderly mob. Armed only with "such as I have," these distributors of God's provision were mystified.

We also realize that after the brokenness, we will only be capable of sharing "such as we have." The glory is that "such as you have" will be more than enough. It will satisfy the longing of others. What they will receive from your hands will have been touched by the Master. As stated previously, anything man-made will need to be broken to serve the purposes of God. As we allow God to break us, we become more for the multitudes.

Presently and sadly, it would seem that much of what is being touted as the Word of God is nothing more than the words of men and women with a veneer of truth. How do I know this? Because many who receive those words are still hungry and dissatisfied. Jesus always satisfies. We must carefully give others only the part of us broken by His love. Anything else is empty, deceptive, and void of the ability to meet the deepest needs of humanity.

We will often feel that we are inadequate to meet the needs of humanity. As Jesus taught in John 15, apart from Him, we can do nothing. This is even more true when we attempt to solve the issues of life apart from His wisdom and His Word. Face it, if we could solve the problems apart from Him, we as a human race would have done so by now. That is the heart of secular humanism—life without God.

Realizing our inadequacy is not being negative or faithless. It's a true statement that unleashes God's grace. The Apostle Paul stated, "I would rather boast of my weaknesses that the power of Christ would rest upon me" (2 Corinthians 12:9). This was from a man among the most spiritual men of his day and one of the best educated. He sat at the feet of the legendary Gamaliel; He probably spoke five languages and had the equivalent of two PhDs. But he would rather boast of his weakness that the power of Christ would be seen.

That's humility. That's recognizing which side of the bread is buttered. We can do all things ... through Christ. More remarkable is the One in you. He makes you great through your union with Him. In realizing these fundamental truths, you discover the ability to do more for more people with less.

Reflection Questions

How should acknowledging your dependence on God, as described above influence your sense of humility and gratitude in daily life?

In what ways can realizing your union with God enable you to achieve more with a diminished reliance on self?

Reflect on a time when recognizing a fundamental truth about yourself or your capabilities allowed you to make a significant, positive impact on others. How did this realization change your approach to helping others?

Chapter 19

I Want To See Jesus

In Luke 24, there is an account of the post-Resurrection Jesus walking for several miles with some disciples without them recognizing Him. He was arguably the most famous person in the region, but Jesus' walking mates did not know who He was. Remarkable. Impossible. Scary. It's scary to think that we could walk and talk with the Son of God yet be oblivious to who He is. This was the case of the two disciples who remained nameless.

They had a conversation with Jesus on the road to Emmaus. Jesus confounded them. Their own testimony was that their hearts burned within them when He spoke. His speech was so pure. His words were the Word. Of course, their hearts burned within them.

Have you been in a service and the preacher spoke in such a way that your heart was moved? You knew that it was not just their ability to communicate the phrases used or even how the presentation was made. But you knew something or "someone" was in the midst but you didn't know what that was. I think this happens often, but rather than realizing it is His presence, we either discount it or give the glory to a person's oratory skills with the Scriptures.

They failed to recognize that Jesus was in their midst while walking on the road with Him. The person that Jesus was talking about was Himself, which is why their hearts burned upon hearing His words. Too often in our post-modern Christian circles, we celebrate the Scriptures and the speaker but fail to see the Living Word.

Jesus seemed to test them by continuing on His journey when one of them persuaded Him to stay the night. Oh, that we would, once again, convince Jesus to stay with us. To sit with Him and Him to dine with us. When Jesus broke the bread, their eyes were opened. They saw Jesus. There is a profound revelation within that idea.

Breaking the bread of life exposes the Master to us and in us. The breaking of bread is when we gradually remove the scales from our eyes. We go from those walking with Christ to those who abide in Christ and He in us. We move from spectators who gossip about someone else's experience to worshipers because we have encountered the living Christ. We tasted. We saw it, and it was good.

What you need is an encounter with Jesus, not "church," indeed not religion, but with Jesus, the King of the Kingdom. As you meet Him on your Emmaus road, you will have something to talk about. As the bread was broken, so must we be broken. Let me reiterate, though, that the brokenness that speaks to God's work within you is neither the brokenness you experience as a consequence of sin nor is it a result of the vicissitudes of life.

Instead, it's a brokenness of the spirit of self, wherein you come to recognize the Lordship of Jesus and allow the "treasure in earthen vessels" to be placed front and center, on display for the world to see. The excellency is of God and from God. But it is only realized as the calloused heart, even of the religious, is shattered on the altar of Him who is altogether lovely.

Even Doctor Luke records in Acts 4:42 four essential aspects of apostolic doctrine: teaching, fellowship, the breaking of bread, and prayers. The apostles' doctrine deals with the things that the apostles taught—what they believed, what they heard while in the presence of the Lord Jesus Christ, and what they saw. Fellowship is a much deeper concept than what is used by the post-modern church. Fellowship (koinonia) was more than a church picnic or a gathering to sing a few songs; rather, it spoke of joint participation or partnership—an intimacy of life.

As the saying goes, the family that prays together stays together. These prayers, often offered outside, were the lifeline from believer to God and believer to believer. Intimacy, in part, is achieved with whom you pray, to whom you pray, and for whom you pray. The phrase 'breaking of bread' was pretty typical. Understanding its meaning largely depended upon the context in which it was used. When used in the context of a meal, it simply meant sharing bread or food. However, in the absence of a larger meal and situated in the context of worship, 'the breaking of bread' refers to the Lord's Supper. Seeing Jesus in our lives only occurs as He breaks us.

Reflection Questions

Reflect on the story of the two disciples on the road to Emmaus. How does their initial failure to recognize Jesus challenge your perception of how He may be present in your own life?

Consider Jesus breaking bread with the disciples as a moment of revelation for them. How might breaking bread symbolize spiritual awakening and recognition of Christ's presence in our lives?

Explore the concept of brokenness as a pathway to intimacy with God. How does the idea of being broken from the spirit of self resonate with you? Reflect on how embracing a posture of brokenness can lead to a deeper understanding of God's grace and a more profound encounter with His presence in your life.

Chapter 20

I Saw it in My Own Life

At age 14, I went away to high school. Living away from home as a young teen around people who didn't look or talk like me was challenging. Through that experience, the greater good was released within me. It was in that place I became a two-time all-American soccer player. Then I was accepted to Brown University, the number one university in the country. I found Jesus at Brown, or I should say, Jesus found me on December 4, 1981—the same night I was planning to take my life.

Fast forward many years. I was in the midst of a divorce, experienced the suicide of a personal friend, suffered from personal depression, and was on four medications while pastoring a growing church. I was serving on no less than ten community/civic boards, and working toward two advanced degrees—a doctorate (with a grade point average of 3.95) and a master's in public administration from Harvard.

Even after 500 people left the Cathedral of Life Christian Assembly, the church I founded, taking with them their financial resources, we were able to buy a historic church building. There is no way I could take credit for or think that somehow it was my ability. It couldn't have been. I was drugged up, and I was hurting in more ways than I can remember. I could barely think straight.

Nevertheless, more was accomplished in that broken phase of my life than when I was "whole." But God, who takes the foolish things and confounds the wise, had already pronounced the blessing on my life. He eulogized me while I was yet living in my mother's womb and said "You, Jeffery, shall not die, but live. You, Jeffery, shall overcome and recover all." Brokenness releases a level of blessing that might otherwise die unrealized. Brokenness removes any sense of personal capability and allows the grace of God to reign supreme amid chaos for the God-breathed "eulogy" to come to pass in our lives.

Testimonies are easy to tell, but are often difficult seasons to live through. Just like the crumbled pieces of bread that were the aftermath of Jesus breaking the loaves contained the impact of Jesus' blessing (eulogy), the blessing of God remained on my life despite what I was experiencing. And as I stated before, the breaking doesn't disqualify you from the blessing; it serves to surface the hidden potential and power necessary to transform the lives of many—most importantly, your own life.

Reflection Question

Reflect on the challenges and adversities you've faced in your own life. Have you experienced moments where you felt overwhelmed by circumstances yet somehow found the strength and resilience to persevere?

Consider the role of faith and divine intervention in your journey. Have there been moments when you recognized God's presence and guidance, even amid difficult times? Reflect on how your faith has sustained you through trials and shaped your perspective on life's challenges.

Explore the concept of brokenness as a catalyst for transformation and blessing. How does my testimony resonate with your understanding of how God works in the lives of believers?

Chapter 21

Are We There Yet?

Have you arrived at the place called broken yet? There is a vast difference between being broken by sin or life and being broken because you realize your sinfulness. One means you're suffering because of consequences, while the other may not have any outward causes, yet inwardly you recognize you are quite a mess. All sin can be summed up in this statement "doing (even thinking) anything apart from what God wants."

You were bought with the blood of Jesus; thus, you are not your own. You can't just do what you want, go where you want, think what you want, hate who you wish to, drink, eat, smoke, and so on. Your money is not yours, any more than the breath in your body is yours. It's all His. Failure to appreciate and honor His ownership of you is a sin.

I'm not attempting to make you feel bad about your sins because the brokenness that is required has little to do with the sins you commit but rather the overall condition of your heart toward God.

Your sin is just a reflection of your heart. Your actions reveal who you listen to and what you believe. Sin, often expressed as an action, is a by-product of what you think and who you believe. So this study in brokenness is helping you look in the mirror to your face and staring at it so you can see yourself as you are, not as you think or hope you are.

Why is this important, you ask? Because our failure to be honest with ourselves has led us into the present condition we now find ourselves. It's a self-deception that has spoiled so much of our past. And if we want the manifestation of God in our lives, it will require a serious look at ourselves first.

One word of caution: We often spend time hearing or reading a message like this, which causes us to think about someone else. We take this information and load up our spiritual guns and get on our spiritual high horse to blow someone else away—rather than weeping over the Word of the Lord and examining ourselves first. Didn't Jesus say, "First take the beam or log out of your eye, then you can see more clearly how to remove the speck from your brother's or sister's eye" (Matthew 7:3)?

Brokenness positions you to receive more of Him rather than being preoccupied with yourself. It's an invitation to experience a joy with which this world can never compete. You will enjoy strength and clarity that evade most believers. If you hear this message from the Lord today, God will lift you to a new level you have never known before. Your hope will return. Your prayer life and boldness will take a new form. You will stop worshiping at the altar of what could and should have been. And you will return to the secret sweet place in God—a place where tears of joy flow, where faith overwhelms and fear ends.

This revelation about brokenness is for those who have had enough, who are dissatisfied with life—their present situation, their home life, their social life, their spiritual life, and even their church life. This message addresses those hungry for God's genuine, authentic move *and* who are willing to do what it takes to experience it. You cry but no relief comes. You try to pray, yet nothing happens. You are between the proverbial rock and a hard place with nowhere to go.

It's through brokenness that we experience God's fullness. It sounds counterintuitive to think that brokenness brings wholeness. But remember, His ways are not our ways. The truth is that the eulogy or blessing will not manifest in our lives until we submit to the breaking by the hands of Jesus. A God-broken life is a life prepared for God's fullness. But, as I have stated earlier, brokenness doesn't mean being destitute. Without the touch of God, we will continue to live well below our privilege.

Reflection Questions

Reflect on the concept of brokenness as described in the chapter. Do you see a distinction between being broken by sin or life's circumstances and being broken because of recognizing your sinfulness?

Consider the idea that sin is a reflection of the condition of our hearts toward God. How does this perspective challenge you to examine your thoughts, beliefs, and actions?

Explore the invitation to experience joy and strength through brokenness. Have you ever experienced moments of brokenness that ultimately led to a more profound sense of God's presence and peace?

Chapter 22

Signs of True Brokenness

In this state of brokenness, we lose sight of ourselves, or at least we realize that we are not the center of the universe. As the Apostle Paul wrote, may we be found in Him, not having a righteousness of our own (see Philippians 3:3-7). The flesh, its beauty and accomplishments, is nothing in light of who He is Jesus Christ glorious. Our challenge has been thinking that the issues of life bring brokenness. In one sense, the brokenness that the heavens recognize only comes as a result of seeing ourselves in light of who He is.

Again, the brokenness I'm referring to doesn't occur because of circumstances. Brokenness, which is irresistible to God, is always based upon a revelation of who He is. In the sinful life of King David, when He saw his grievous sin juxtaposed to the mercy of God, he exclaimed, "A broken spirit, a broken spirit, and contrite heart thou will not despise" (Psalm 51:17). Strangely, even our attempts at showing God our humility and how sorry we are fail until we see Him. His amazing grace will melt the proudest hearted. His mercy will bring to their knees any who behold Him.

Brokenness—true brokenness—causes a feeling of sorrow for our spiritual ignorance and that of others as well. It's not based upon the idea that they are "dumb," but instead they feel for their loss of relationship due to the lack of brokenness. Instead of judging or throwing rocks, why not call a one-person intercessory prayer meeting for the fallen or troubled? We are not broken, as God would have us, until our hearts break over what breaks His heart.

Brokenness leaves no room for gossip or holding grudges. This personal understanding of how much we have been forgiven causes us to love God and humanity deeply. A broken person yields more to the way of God, the will of God, and the heart of God—and submits to the Word of God. They feel their sin. They sense when they are off and hurt them because they allow nothing to get between their relationship with God and them.

Reflection Questions

Reflect on the idea that true brokenness is not primarily based on external circumstances but on discovering who God is. How does this perspective challenge your understanding of brokenness?

Consider King David's response in Psalm 51 when confronted with his sin. How does David's recognition of his spiritual ignorance and need for God's mercy resonate with you? Reflect on how moments of brokenness in your own life have led to a deeper understanding of your need for God's grace and forgiveness.

Explore the transformative impact of brokenness on our attitudes and actions toward others. How does brokenness lead to a greater compassion for those who are spiritually lost or struggling?

Chapter 23

What Brokenness Is Not

Brokenness is not an inferiority complex masquerading as humility or piety. It is not walking around penniless or bowed over, staring at the ground. Brokenness is not lamenting over all the ills that may have befallen you. Brokenness is not constantly reliving the regret and shame of your past sin. In truth, sin is a manifestation of a lack of brokenness.

A person who lives with the revelation of God's mercy and grace yields more readily to the Word of God. Sin, especially sins of commission, become less frequent, for a genuine fear of God abides with a broken person. If brokenness were a result of experiencing the storms of life, then most of the world, even the Church, would be broken. But what is true is that being hurt and broken are different. Brokenness is a condition from which you don't want to recover, for it is in this state of brokenness that His glory is revealed in and through you.

In the text of Mark 6, it is only after the breaking of the bread that Jesus began to feed the multitude through the distribution channel of His disciples. Our brokenness enables us to be "more" for the needs of the people. The full potential of the bread could not be realized until the breaking occurred. The same holds for you. Full potential (unlimited) cannot be realized until you are broken. Until you cease to exist in your present, self-made state and submit to the reduction process, you will never see the fruitfulness that is your destiny. If there's no personal brokenness, there's no miracle ability to help others. This is the heart of this message: you are broken by the revelation of who Jesus is and what He accomplished on your behalf. In the coming to the end of yourself, His life begins.

An area in which we may not be experiencing brokenness is in our relationships. How can we serve the world when we are not serving the members of our own spiritual house or community? The adage charity begins at home is accurate. I'm sure that statement applies to your immediate home or family but I want us to think about the church community for a minute.

Years ago, there was a popular commercial whose famous line was "where's the beef?" I want to ask a different question, however, and that is "where's the love?" Undoubtedly, the people who take a message like this to heart usually do all they know to do to show love to everyone. The most critical ones show less love than others.

That said, my challenge to you is to allow the

Holy Spirit to deal with you and teach you how to relate to others. Do you pray for others? Or do you gossip about others? Are you forgiving, or are you self-righteous and condemning? You cannot serve with the Holy Spirit if you cannot forgive others. If you cannot love others who may not be lovable at this moment, then you aren't serving with the love of Jesus.

Our brokenness leads to greater effectiveness of service. How can you carry around with grudges, offenses, and ill feelings in your heart toward others in the family and still expect God to answer your cries for help, deliverance, blessing, and prosperity? Although you don't earn a relationship with God through Christ, you maintain it by loving others as Christ has loved and forgiven you. What did John the Beloved say? "How can you say you love God, whom you have not seen, but hate your brother, whom you see every day?" (1 John 4:20).

Reflection Questions

Reflect on the misconception that brokenness is a display of inferiority or self-pity. How does the chapter challenge this notion and redefine brokenness as a condition of yielding to God's mercy and grace?

Explore the analogy in Mark 6 of the breaking of bread as a metaphor for spiritual brokenness. How does the chapter emphasize that true potential and fruitfulness can only be realized through submission to the process of brokenness?

Consider the importance of love and forgiveness in fostering genuine brokenness and service within the church community. How does this chapter highlight the connection between brokenness and relational harmony?

Chapter 24

Broken People

When Jesus went ashore, He saw a large crowd [waiting], and He was moved with compassion for them because they were like sheep without a shepherd [lacking guidance]; and He began to teach them many things. When the day was nearly gone, His disciples came to Him and said, "This is an isolated place, and it is already late; send the crowds away so that they may go into the surrounding countryside and villages and buy themselves something to eat." But He replied, "You give them something to eat!" And they asked Him, "Shall we go and buy 200 denarii worth of bread and give it to them to eat?" He said to them, "How many loaves do you have? Go look!" And when they found out, they said, "Five [loaves], and two fish." Then Jesus commanded them all to sit down by groups on the green grass. They sat down in groups of hundreds and of fifties

> *[so that the crowd resembled an orderly arrangement of colorful garden plots]. Taking the five loaves and two fish, He looked up to heaven and said a blessing [of praise and thanksgiving to the Father]. Then He broke the loaves and [repeatedly] gave them to the disciples to set before the people; and He divided up the two fish among them all. They all ate and were satisfied.*
> – Mark 6:34-42

As a people who are part of a church, we tend to see the work of ministry as getting a job done or performing a task, like serving in an area of ministry such as teaching, ushering, music, prison, etc. But the activities of the ministry are not the same as ministering to the Lord or ministering to another. Jesus died to restore relationship and fellowship with the Father. Restoring people was the heart, the mission, the goal of His incarnation. He did not come to establish a religion, wearing collars and vestments. He was not buying property and building places today known as churches.

One cannot be a Christian alone. Your walk requires a relationship with others to be a fully actualized follower of Jesus. Solo Christianity doesn't work any more than a hand can function without the rest of the body. Being a child of God means you are part of a royal family with brothers, sisters, and spiritual parents. God has designed His Church in such a way that unless you work to remain vitally connected to your spiritual family members, you will be less than you can be, and all the other members of His body will suffer as they are deprived of your presence.

In his letter to the church in Ephesus, the Apostle Paul wrote, "Endeavor to keep the unity of the spirit in the bond of peace" (Ephesians 4:3). This lack of unity in the bond of peace is precisely why many of us are weak, sick, and dying prematurely, as described in 1 Corinthians 11:29. That occurs because we are not discerning, understanding, or appreciating the necessity of adequately relating to one another. Ignoring each other, talking about one another, holding grudges, failing to pray, care for, or even recognize the value of your fellow Christian are the reasons you can't go to the next dimension in your relationship with Jesus.

The Bible commands us to break up the fallow ground (see Hosea 10:12). That's an agricultural term that describes a plot of land that has not been tilled or prepared to receive fresh, clean seed. Breaking and allowing the Word to penetrate and then to bring forth fruit in your life requires a willingness to pull up the stumps, remove the rocks, and soften the soil. There can be no harvest until you're not ready to receive and obey the Word of God. Most believers want Jesus to help them feel better and go to heaven. To be a follower and disciple, however, is challenging; it requires sacrifice and humility.

Reflection Questions

Reflect on the distinction between performing ministry tasks and genuinely ministering to the Lord and others. How does this perspective challenge familiar notions of church involvement and service?

Explore the analogy of the body of Christ and the importance of relational connection within the church community. Reflect on the implications of solo Christianity and the necessity of remaining vitally connected to other believers for spiritual growth and well-being.

Consider breaking up fallow ground as a metaphor for preparing yourself to receive the Word of God. Reflect on areas in your life where the soil of your heart may need to be softened and cultivated to allow for spiritual growth and transformation.

Chapter 25

He Only Uses Broken People

Jesus only gave what was broken and blessed, not what was just blessed. A eulogy speaks of blessing, which speaks of empowerment. But what people need is the part of you that God breaks. People who are just broken by life but not by the revelation of Jesus Christ will be bitter servants—nasty, angry, and raw, ministering out of their experiences rather than from the comfort and grace of God they have received.

When my daughters were young, and they allowed me to make their lunches for school, I would remove the crust of the peanut butter and jelly sandwiches, especially for Princess Grace. It took a little longer to get everyone ready for school, but the crust wasn't as crucial to her little taste buds as the creamy Skippy and Welch's grape jelly! I know that's silly, but the fact is that until you allow your crusty self to be cut away, others will not be able to taste and see that the Lord is good. They will never get to the good stuff in you—and neither will you,

The broken part won't have a whole lot of ego, grudges, or titles. People don't need the part of your unsubmitted, unconsecrated, uncircumcised personality; they need to be nourished by the part of you that God has transformed. Anytime someone says, "Well, that's just the way I am," they are telling us they are not submitted to God. They are saying that their self is superior to God's Word.

Furthermore, they are stating, in no uncertain terms, that no one can correct or instruct them. The educated, athletic, intellectual, talented, and gifted person is not what others want. What they need, the bread they need, is the part of you that is saturated in the presence of God, transformed by a confrontation with the Miracle-Working One. They don't crave your title, position, or personal consecration. They need the part of you that limps like Jacob limped after wrestling with the angel of the Lord, the part of you that is transformed like Saul was after seeing a great light and becoming Paul. That's what others want. That's what they need. People desperately need your transformed self, even a self that is in the transformation process—not your unconsecrated mind filled with your thoughts but God's thoughts through you. Brokenness is required.

A good example of this is when someone breaks a physical bone, and that bone heals incorrectly. The orthopedic surgeon will often have to reset or re-break the bone so it can heal properly, never to break again in the same place. Doctor

Jesus is the best orthopedic surgeon there is. He was there when you were being formed in your mother's womb.

Often, people give others the results or the residue of the rough things that have occurred in their lives. The bread that they are serving is often stale, bitter, hard, and crummy. Although things happen in life that can break you, unless those things get touched by the Master, you will not only remain busted up but will share your misery, not the ministry of grace, with others.

Sometimes, when people become parents, they teach their children things from a place of pain, parenting from a wounded, unhealed emotional place. So, instead of giving their children and friends wisdom, they impart fear and distrust to them. Because they got hurt as a wife, they give the bread of distrust to their daughters. Because they failed in business or the "man messed them over," they teach their sons not to trust anyone who doesn't look like them. They got hurt in the church by a fellow Christian, a leader, or even their pastor. Then, upon returning home, they spread their hurt in an attempt to protect them.

When they do that, they are not feeding their children healthy bread. They're feeding them stale, moldy wheat. Then they are surprised when their kids, and even their spouse, don't want Jesus or have respect for authority—adults, teachers, elders, and pastors. God hates gossipers, talebearers, and strife-makers. Like Moses interceded on behalf of his sister Miriam, a prophetess, when she and Aaron, the first high priest, questioned Moses' ability to hear God's voice correctly because of His choice of a wife. God rebuked them for their gossip and murmuring. God struck Miriam with leprosy and evicted her from the camp, away from His presence.

I have similarly feared for some of God's people, for I see the same attitude in them that was in Miriam and Aaron. God was not pleased with those two and now He isn't pleased with people who act like them. How can you judge another man's servant? The Apostle Paul reported that Alexander the coppersmith had done him much harm. Paul prayed that the Lord would repay him (see 2 Timothy 4:14). Even Jesus had a Judas who betrayed Him. A "Judas" will always self-destruct. It's just a matter of time.

Why are you in your neighbor's business? Why are you so interested in someone else's life and world? You need to wake up and look around you. Things are serious out there. Many of the young, rich, powerful, and famous are dying. The so-called saved are dying. Millions of people are out of work, families are disintegrating, and kids are confused emotionally and sexually. More people are working but still don't have enough to eat. Churches are closing at an alarming rate. More Christians are sick than ever before, and more people are depressed and killing themselves in epidemic proportions.

Why do you have any time to be in somebody's business? Check your own life. Make your life a reality show and study what you should do. In most families, only one person might be attending church. Some can't get breakthroughs in their homes because they have unwittingly ushered in the anti-Christ spirit of division into their relationships. People are destroying others with their words, which is not love.

It doesn't matter how holy you think you are; the Bible says that a man who can bridle or control his tongue is a mature person (see James 1:26). The Bible says blessed are the peacemakers (not the trouble makers). They are empowered to prosper, for they shall be called the sons of God (see Matthew 5:9).

Some then decide to leave a church, which may not be a bad idea, but the problem is they are leaving with their unbroken self. Furthermore, they justify their leaving and spread poison to others. Don't think God is okay with that. Don't think there isn't judgment that comes into a life because of that.

If we are spiritually mature, we are to restore our fallen brother or sister. We can help the hurting, cover the confused, and pray for the afflicted. That's the Bible, my friend, that's the Bible.

Reflection Question

Reflect on the concept of brokenness in regards to serving others. Consider how allowing God to break you can transform bitterness and anger into comfort and grace for them.

Explore the metaphor of cutting away the crust to access the core of one's being. Reflect on areas of your life where the "crust" needs to be removed to reveal the true essence transformed by God.

Consider the impact of parenting or influencing others from a place of pain and woundedness. Reflect on how unresolved issues can affect relationships and perpetuate negative stereotypes.

Chapter 26

Jesus Blessed What He Broke and Gave Only What Was Broken

What Jesus gave the disciples the food to distribute to the multitudes, the food was blessed and then broken. We must be broken before we can be of spiritual value to others—including ourselves. We need to be broken of our selfishness, our prideful ways and attitudes, our excuses, our self-righteousness and judgmental attitudes, our unforgiveness, and our "I know that already" arrogance. And yes, we need to be broken of the attitude that allows us to hold grudges against others—especially those within the body of Christ.

Because of this lack of brokenness you are ineffective in releasing the God-kind of life to others and do not realize your prayers are being hindered the whole time. Still, others must be broken from their carnal and sinful ways and habits. The habit of making excuses for poor behavior kills more dreams than any one thing I know—no more excuses. Just admit and confess your weaknesses and sins to God. Receive forgiveness and learn how to remain free.

The Bible reminds us that in the last days, men will gather to themselves, teachers who will tickle their ears. If you want to tickle, buy a Tickle-Me-Elmo doll. When Peter stood up to preach on the day of Pentecost, even after denying Jesus Christ three times, it pierced the hearts of the religious leaders of his day. They wanted to prevent him from doing that. Until we are broken, we are not much more than a moving mouth with little to no impact on the grand scheme.

The heart of brokenness occurs when you give up your life, such as it is, and receive His life. And it is at this point that Jesus can share you with the world around you. Do you really want salvation to come to your house, to your job, to your campus, to your ministry? Then fall on the rock called Christ Jesus. Forget others in terms of what they are saying or will say about you. They talked about Jesus, and they will talk about you as well. Brokenness is the beginning of health and healing for you and those with whom you come in contact.

The impact of Jesus was not known until He died on the cross for all humanity—past, present, and future. Though Jesus performed countless miracles, it wasn't until He was "broken" that the work of redemption could commence. The text reads, "I tell you that unless a grain of wheat that falls to the ground dies, it stays just a grain; but if it dies, it produces a big harvest" (John 12:24, CJB).

There is no lack of references that speak of the necessity of Jesus' suffering on our behalf. But as we read further, it's equally clear that His followers must also deny themselves and give up their way of doing life to be true disciples with tremendous impact. Jesus responded to those who thought that He should not die the death of a criminal by informing them of the cost of following Him:

> "If anyone wishes to follow Me [as My disciple], he must deny himself [set aside selfish interests], and take up his cross [expressing a willingness to endure whatever may come] and follow Me [believing in Me, conforming to My example in living and, if need be, suffering or perhaps dying because of faith in Me]" (Mark 8:34).

Brokenness is the way of discipleship. To embrace this is the beginning of a fruitful life and personal ministry. It is a fallacy of the modern church to think there is a blessing without breaking, glory without suffering, and triumph without trials. This view has created spiritually anemic generations that lack grit and the ability to thrive amid difficulties. If that devil can't stop you from progressing, a life of ease will do the job. We have become a microwave Church, demanding that everything we want or need happen with the snap of a finger. No waiting, no preparation. Just put it in the microwave, wait one minute, and there it is—an instant blessed life with power, authority, prosperity, healing, and salvation.

Reflection Questions

How does the concept of brokenness contribute to spiritual value and effectiveness in ministry? Reflect on selfishness, pride, judgmental attitudes, and unforgiveness in your life, and consider how embracing brokenness can lead to a more significant impact in serving others.

Reflect on embracing the cost of discipleship, as seen in Jesus' willingness to suffer and die for humanity. Consider the sacrifices and challenges involved in following Jesus wholeheartedly and how you can align your life more closely with His example.

Consider embracing trials and difficulties as integral to the Christian journey. Reflect on how a culture of instant gratification can hinder spiritual growth and resilience and how you can cultivate perseverance and endurance in your faith walk.

Chapter 27

A Broken Revelation

The significance of brokenness extends beyond personal introspection; it penetrates to the very core of our faith. In a world inundated with social media preachers and fleeting TikTok revelations, the absence of brokenness among those who lead leaves a profound impact. As the Apostle Paul lamented in 2 Timothy 3:7, many are "ever learning and never able to come to a precise and experiential knowledge of the truth." Our pursuit of truth has been compromised by second- or third-hand knowledge, unchecked against the Word of God. This unchecked information festers, distorting our understanding of grace, sin, and redemption.

At stake is the purity of the Gospel itself. Our theology becomes distorted without embracing brokenness, resulting in shallow spirituality and misguided beliefs. Our witness to the world loses its authenticity, and we become hypocrites preaching a Gospel we haven't fully embraced. Our lives fail to reflect the transformative power of Christ, diminishing our impact on society.

Brokenness is not a burden but a gift—a pathway to true intimacy with God, genuine spiritual growth, and practical ministry. It unlocks the fullness of our faith, enabling us to fulfill God's calling in our lives. Through brokenness, we find healing, restoration, and the abundant life promised by Christ.

It seems to be a contradiction in terms to say that by becoming less, you can do more. But that's exactly what is possible when you yield to the process of brokenness at the hands of the Master. This type of brokenness isn't a one-time experience, one and done. But rather it's an ongoing process that yields more and more fruit over time.

I'm reminded of the parable in John 15:2 when Jesus taught that in order to be more fruitful, pruning is required. The pruning process is tantamount to the breaking process. Growth requires a temporary dismantling of yourself. Therefore, embrace brokenness wholeheartedly, recognizing it as the catalyst for profound transformation in your life and in the world around you.

Reflection Questions

How has the absence of brokenness among spiritual leaders impacted your understanding of faith and the Gospel message?

Reflect on a time when unchecked information or second-hand knowledge distorted your understanding of grace, sin, or redemption. How did this experience affect your spiritual journey?

In what ways can you embrace brokenness as a gift rather than a burden lead to deeper intimacy with God and more effective ministry in your life?

Chapter 28

School's In Session: Six Takeaways on Embracing Brokenness

As we bring this book to a close, let's review some of the more salient points from the previous chapters.

1. Know You're Blessed.

A significant key to turning your life around is recognizing that the Lord has eulogized you before you even experienced brokenness. You are blessed. You have been pre-ordained to prosper, overcome, and achieve more than you can imagine. God's plan for your life is a success, regardless of the difficulties you have experienced. Your past is not a prophecy of your future. Embrace and hold on tightly to this truth, especially in doubt and despair. Remembering your inherent blessings empowers you to face challenges confidently, knowing you are destined for greatness.

2. Recognize More Is Possible.

When you experience setbacks, you can lose sight of your dreams. The debris from the wrecks of bad decisions and thoughtless acts obscures your vision. Depression, regret, and hopelessness are all too familiar emotions. But through the divine breaking process of being reduced to crumbs, you will see that you're not at the end. Your best life is yet ahead of you. Embrace the opportunity for renewal and growth that comes from setbacks. Instead of dwelling on past failures, focus on the limitless possibilities. Allow yourself to dream again, knowing that your future holds infinite potential waiting to be realized.

3. Give What You Are.

You cannot be expected to give what you do not have. You have something to use as a starting point, a seed for more. Give that. Present that. Offer that. That seed is the true you, just as you are. Your unique experiences, talents, and perspectives are valuable gifts you can share with the world. Even in times of brokenness, you still have much to offer. Embrace your authenticity and allow it to shine through in everything you do. By giving from the heart, you sow positivity and transformation, yielding a bountiful harvest in due time.

4. Submit to the Breaking Process.

Becoming more is a voluntary, intentional act that begins with submitting to the process. It's a process that the Master, your Creator, controls and has tailored especially for you. No process, no progress. Know the process and experience progress. Surrendering to the breaking process can be challenging but essential for growth and transformation. Trust in the wisdom of the Master and allow Him to mold you into the person He created you to be. Embrace each step of the journey, knowing that every trial and tribulation shapes you into a stronger, more resilient individual.

5. Keep Giving.

Giving is the key to living. Continue to position yourself for the Master's touch and to be utilized to serve others. You won't ever be used up; you will increase your capacity to give and impact the lives of others for their betterment. The more you give, the more you receive in return. Cultivate a spirit of generosity and abundance, knowing that every act of kindness can make a difference in someone else's life. Trust in the universe's abundance and give freely of yourself, knowing that your contributions will ripple outwards, creating positive change in the world.

6. Expect To Have More and Be More.

You get what you expect. You have no right to expect what you don't expect. Expect this breaking process to yield excellent results in your spiritual walk, affecting other aspects of your life. Approach each day with anticipation and excitement, knowing that more extraordinary things are in store for you. By expecting abundance and growth, you align yourself with the limitless potential of God's universe. Embrace a mindset of positivity and optimism, and watch as opportunities unfold before you. Your expectations shape your reality, so dare to dream big and believe that the best is yet to come.

Chapter 29

Ten Insights To Embracing Brokenness

The Word of God is like a multifaceted diamond. When a diamond is exposed to light, it reveals its brilliance through numerous reflections and refractions, each facet offering a unique perspective on its beauty. Similarly, the Word of God, when illuminated by the Holy Spirit, unveils deeper truths and insights that are critical for our spiritual growth and understanding. This divine illumination enables us to comprehend the complexities and purposes of the various experiences we encounter, particularly the role of brokenness in our lives.

Just as a diamond is formed under immense pressure and heat, our character and faith are strengthened through adversity. The Holy Spirit guides us to see that our moments of brokenness are not indications of failure or abandonment, but are instead part of God's transformative process, designed to bring forth our hidden strengths and potentials. By embracing this perspective, we can find hope and purpose even in the most difficult seasons of our lives, trusting that God's blessing remains with us at it shapes us into vessels of His grace and power. Here are some things to remembers in the midst of your brokenness.

1. Know your purpose and power are still in you, despite being broken.

Even in moments of brokenness, understanding that your purpose and power remain within you is crucial. Recognizing this truth empowers you to navigate through challenges with resilience and determination. Your inherent purpose and strength persist despite the fractures and setbacks, guiding you toward growth and renewal.

2. Everything changes in the Master's hands.

Entrusting your broken pieces to the Master's hands brings transformation and restoration. Just as a skilled artisan can mend shattered pottery into a beautiful masterpiece, so can the Master mend your brokenness into something magnificent. Surrendering to His guidance and wisdom leads to healing and fulfilling His perfect plan for your life.

3. Your future looks better than your past.

Despite the pain of brokenness, your future promises renewal and redemption. While trials and tribulations may mark the past, they do not dictate what lies ahead. Embrace hope for a brighter tomorrow, filled with new opportunities, growth, and blessings beyond measure.

4. Yielding what you have is the beginning of having more.

Letting go of what you hold onto allows abundance to flow into your life. By releasing your grip on the broken fragments of the past, you open yourself up to receive more incredible blessings and opportunities. Yielding what you have is the first step towards experiencing the fullness of the future.

5. Your best is still possible.

Despite experiencing brokenness, your potential for greatness remains intact. Brokenness does not diminish your capacity to achieve your dreams or make a positive impact. Instead, it catalyzes growth and resilience, and enables you to realize your highest potential.

6. More happens when you become less.

True abundance is found in selflessness and humility. When you prioritize serving others and putting their needs above your own, you experience a profound sense of fulfillment and purpose. By becoming less focused on yourself and more focused on others, you create space for miracles to unfold and blessings to abound.

7. You have more to give after being blessed.

The blessings you receive are meant to be shared with others. As you experience God's grace and provision, you are called to be a conduit of His love and generosity. By giving freely of what you have been blessed with, you amplify the impact of those blessings and spread hope and joy to those around you.

8. Don't minimize what you have to start with.

Even the smallest of beginnings can lead to extraordinary outcomes. Do not underestimate the value of what you offer, no matter how insignificant it may seem. Every talent, resource, and opportunity are gifts to be cherished and utilized to their fullest potential.

9. It's still up to you.

Despite your challenges and obstacles, the power to overcome lies within you. You must take ownership of your circumstances and chart a course towards a brighter future. You can transcend adversity and create your desired life by embracing resilience, determination, and faith.

10. There's wholeness in brokenness

Paradoxically, amid brokenness, there exists the potential for profound wholeness. By embracing and healing your brokenness, you discover a more profound sense of authenticity, empathy, and connection with yourself and others. Acknowledging and embracing your brokenness are the pathways to true wholeness and fulfillment.

Chapter 30

The Journey From Brokenness To Purposeful Transformation

Transitioning from brokenness to purposeful transformation is not a journey that occurs overnight. Instead, it is a gradual process that unfolds over time. While a moment of chaos may catalyze this journey, true transformation requires patience and perseverance as you navigate the challenges and obstacles. As discussed earlier, the process of breaking that leads to holy transformation is deeply rooted in an ongoing revelation of God's nature and your identity in light of His glory.

Throughout the Bible, we encounter individuals whose lives were radically transformed by their encounters with the glory of God. Their responses to these divine encounters are testimonies to the transformative power of beholding His Majesty. Consider Isaiah, who, upon seeing the Lord seated on His throne, cried out, "Woe is me! For I am lost; for I am a man of unclean lips, and I dwell amid a people of unclean lips; for my eyes have seen the King, the LORD of hosts!" (Isaiah 6:5). Isaiah's response reflects a deep sense of humility and repentance in the presence of God's holiness. Isaiah was broken and undone by His vision of who the Lord is and who Isaiah was. That was what qualified him for ministry.

Similarly, when Moses encountered God at the burning bush, he was filled with awe and reverence, hiding his face in fear of the divine presence (see Exodus 3:6). Job, upon encountering God amid his suffering, humbled himself and repented, acknowledging his limitations and inadequacies (see Job 42:5-6). Even the disciples, who walked closely with Jesus during His earthly ministry, were stunned and amazed when they witnessed His turning water into wine, the transfiguration, and His bodily resurrection. Their initial disbelief gave way to awe and wonder as they encountered the risen Christ (see Luke 24:36-37).

These examples remind you that encountering God's glory has a transformative effect on your life. It humbles you, convicts you of sin, and leads you to repentance. It fills you with awe and wonder, inspiring you to live lives that bring glory to His name. As you continue your journey from brokenness to purposeful transformation, may you seek God's presence with earnestness and humility, knowing that He alone has the power to transform our lives from the inside out as the Scriptures confirm in multiple instances:

1. Revelation 1:17 (John's vision on Patmos): "When I saw him, I fell at his feet as though dead. Then he placed his right hand on me and said: 'Do not be afraid. I am the First and the Last'" (NIV).

2. Exodus 3:6 (Moses and the burning bush): "Then he said, 'I am the God of your father, the God of Abraham, the God of Isaac and the God of Jacob.' At this, Moses hid his face, because he was afraid to look at God" (NIV).

3. Job 42:5-6 (Job's response to God's revelation): "My ears had heard of you but now my eyes have seen you. Therefore I despise myself and repent in dust and ashes" (NIV).

4. Luke 5:8 (Peter's encounter with Jesus): "When Simon Peter saw this, he fell at Jesus' knees and said, 'Go away from me, Lord; I am a sinful man!'" (NIV).

5. Luke 24:36-37 (Disciples' reaction to the resurrected Jesus): "While they were still talking about this, Jesus himself stood among them and said to them, 'Peace be with you.' They were startled and frightened, thinking they saw a ghost" (NIV).

People who encounter God with sincerity and

a genuine desire for His presence often experience a profound transformation in their lives. This transformation may not always be as dramatic as the examples in the Bible, but it is no less significant. As we hunger and thirst for God, seeking Him with all our hearts, He reveals Himself to us in deeply personal and transformative ways.

The journey from brokenness to purposeful transformation is not easy. It requires patience, perseverance, and faith. But as you continue to seek God and allow His glory to illuminate your life you will gradually transformed from the inside out. Your heart will be filled with His love, your mind renewed by His truth, and your life empowered by His Spirit.

Ultimately, the transformation process is not just about fixing what is broken but about becoming who you were created to be. It is about embracing your true identity as a beloved child of God and living out His purposes for your life. As you walk this transformation journey, you can trust that God is with you every step of the way, guiding you, strengthening you, and leading you into His glory.

Chapter 31

There's A Master Piece in There

There is a famous quote attributed to Michelangelo regarding his process of sculpting the statue of David. While the exact wording may vary, the essence of the quote is often summarized as follows: "I saw the angel in the marble and carved until I set him free."

According to legend, Michelangelo selected a large block of marble previously worked on by other sculptors but left abandoned. He saw the potential in this flawed piece of marble and believed he could unveil the figure of David within it. Michelangelo worked tirelessly for over two years, carefully chiseling away at the marble to produce the magnificent statue of David that stands over 17 feet tall.

When the statue was finally unveiled in 1504, it was met with great acclaim for its beauty, attention to detail, and the perfect proportions of the human form. Michelangelo's David is admired for its expression of strength, courage, and idealized beauty, becoming an enduring symbol of the Renaissance art movement. Just like this sculpture, the process of breaking that leads to holy transformation is deeply rooted in an ongoing revelation of God's nature in us and our identity in light of His glory.

Like Michelangelo's sculpting, this transformative process is a journey of faith and renewal. As we experience life's challenges and trials, we are shaped and refined by God's loving hands. Each hardship and moment of brokenness are opportunities for divine intervention, where God's grace and mercy work within us to create something beautiful.

Paul, in his letters, referred to this transformative power. In Romans 12:2, he urged the reader, "Do not be conformed to this world, but be transformed by the renewal of your mind, that by testing you may discern what the will of God is, what is good and acceptable and perfect." This transformation is not superficial but produces a profound change that begins within, renewing our minds and aligning our hearts with God's will.

In 2 Corinthians 3:18, Paul elaborated further: "And we all, with unveiled face, beholding the glory of the Lord, are being transformed into the same image from one degree of glory to another. For this comes from the Lord who is the Spirit." This passage highlights that our transformation is an ongoing journey from one degree of glory to another, facilitated by the Spirit of the Lord.

Just as Michelangelo saw the angel within the marble, God sees the potential within each of us;

after all, He put it there. He sees beyond our flaws and imperfections, recognizing the beauty and strength that can emerge through His transformative power. Our role is to trust in His process, surrendering to His hands as He chisels away the rough edges, revealing the masterpiece within.

This process of transformation also involves the Body of Christ—the community of God. God often uses people around us as instruments of His grace. Friends, family, and fellow believers can serve as sources of encouragement, accountability, and support, helping us stay the course and grow in our faith. Proverbs 27:17 says, "As iron sharpens iron, so one person sharpens another." Through meaningful relationships, we are refined and shaped into the image of Christ.

Moreover, God's Word is a vital tool in our transformation. Hebrews 4:12 states, "For the word of God is alive and active. Sharper than any double-edged sword, it penetrates even to dividing soul and spirit, joints and marrow; it judges the thoughts and attitudes of the heart." Scripture guides us, convicts us, and reveals God's character, helping us to grow in holiness and righteousness.

In reflecting on Michelangelo's David and the biblical accounts of transformation, we see a common theme: the journey from brokenness to beauty. This journey requires patience, faith, and perseverance. It involves embracing the chiseling process and trusting that God's intentions are always for our good and His glory.

Ultimately, our transformation is a testimony to the world of God's incredible power and love. As we are changed from within, we reflect His glory to those around us, becoming living examples of His grace. Like the statue of David, our lives can stand as enduring symbols of strength, courage, and the beauty of a life transformed by God's hands.

In summary, the essence of transformation, whether in the hands of a master sculptor or the hands of the Creator, lies in the vision to see beyond the surface, the patience to endure the process, and the faith to believe in the final Master Piece. Through this journey, we become who we were truly meant to be, reflecting the glory and majesty of God in every facet of our lives.

About the Author

Jeffery A. Williams, D.Min., MPA, is the founder and chief empowerment strategist of The Williams Empowerment Group LLC, whose sole mission is to help others achieve their dreams. Having coached more than 1,500 students through multiple coaching programs, live presentations, and interactive webinars, Dr. Williams has earned the reputation of "The Chief Empowerment Officer." A dynamic catalyst to corporations, nonprofit organizations, and entrepreneurs, Dr. Williams draws on his years of experience, education, and insatiable desire to see others "win" to show them how to change the trajectory of their life and business to previously unreached levels.

Dr. Williams has an earned doctorate from Gordon-Conwell Theological Seminary (Urban Complex Settings), a Master's in Public Administration from the Harvard Kennedy School of Government, and a bachelor's degree from Brown University in Social Environmental Analysis. In 2016, Dr. Williams was consecrated a bishop in the Covenant Fellowship Alliance. He and his wife, Lelani, live in Rhode Island and parent two young adult daughters, Joy Victoria and Grace Noelle.

In addition to being a sought-out advisor to members of government, Dr. Williams has been a regular chapel speaker for both the National Football League and Major League Soccer (2005-12, 2014). Dr. Williams is a trained mediator and has published six books: *Knowing Why: The Key That Unlocks Your Full Potential* with a workbook journal (which is used as a college textbook), an ebook entitled, *Resurge: From Disorder to Divine Order in 7 Steps*; and *The Morning Decree Devotionals Journal*--originally published in four volumes.

With a strong desire to educate and elevate members of the community at large, Dr. Williams has dedicated his life to serve as both a spiritual guide and social change advocate. His work as a faith leader began with a nine-person congregation and has since grown to include several hundred members. Internationally he serves as the General Overseer of The Global Ambassadors Leadership Network through which he oversees 60 congregations in twelve nations, including local churches and ministries. His ministry is viewed in 182 nations of the world.

Through both his teachings and his actions, Dr. Williams always leads by example, helping others understand the connection between principle and practice. In 1999, he founded the Cathedral of Life Christian Assembly, renamed The King's Cathedral. He is also the founder of "The Well-Life Project," a funding agency with a mission to create twelve fresh water wells in the African nation of Zambia.

He is the husband of the beautiful Lelani Williams and they are enthusiastic parents to two young adults, Joy Victoria and Grace Noelle Williams. You can learn more about Dr. Williams at www.drjeffwilliams.org. You can also reach Dr. Williams through:

Facebook @williamsglobal777

or via email at

williamsglobal777@gmail.com

www.ingramcontent.com/pod-product-compliance
Lightning Source LLC
LaVergne TN
LVHW051523070426
835507LV00023B/3272